A History of Central Banking
and the Enslavement of Mankind
by
Stephen Mitford Goodson

A History of Central Banking
and the Enslavement of Mankind

by

Stephen Mitford Goodson

1st Edition 2014
2nd Edition 2017
3rd Edition 2017

ISBN-13: 978-1-910881-63-7

Black House Publishing Ltd
Kemp House
152 City Road
London
United Kingdom
EC1V 2NX

www.blackhousepublishing.com
Email: info@blackhousepublishing.com

*And you will never understand American history
or the history of the Occident durin' the past 2000 years
unless you look at one or two problems;
namely, sheenies and usury.
One or the other or BOTH. I should say, both.*

— Ezra Pound

Contents

Foreword

This book is bound to be controversial and engender strong reactions, and I do not endorse all of the viewpoints expressed therein.

Why would a seemingly arid subject matter such as the history of central banking and of the monetary system give rise to such strong reactions? One must wonder why some will attach to this book the stigma of heresy, and argue that Stephen Goodson has gone beyond the parameters of acceptable historical debate.

Goodson has the credentials and track-record to make a credible presentation of a subject matter which he has researched for decades and which he has lived personally as a non-executive Director of the South African Reserve Bank.

I do not have the expertise to say whether Goodson's findings are accurate, but I do know that the raw nerves he touches are on account of central banking and the monetary system created thereunder being at the core of the persistent profound and inhumane differences in wealth distribution within any given country, and among countries.

For this reason, for several years, my Party and I have argued that South Africa should reform its central banking and monetary system, even if that means placing our country out of step with iniquitous world standards.

Books on economics and banking are generally viewed as being abstruse, whose readers are confined mainly to academia and the business world. In this case we have a notable exception.

This work provides not only a broad sweep of the history of economics over almost three millennia, but insights into how the problems of usury have been confounding and enslaving mankind since its civilized existence first began.

It may shock some to realise that central banks throughout the world, including our own South African Reserve Bank, do not serve our own best interests and are in fact in league with private banks. This not only undermines our sovereignty, but deprives us of the means of having publicly-issued debt-free money which belongs to the people as its sovereign debt, and interest-free means of exchange. Instead, in our country, as in other countries, we use private money produced out of debt by the private banking system. Shifting from bank-notes to government-notes would provide our people with a decent life, which is blessed, prosperous and sustainable. But such a simple reform would be a real revolution, more difficult to bring about than any other reform or social change imaginable.

Although South Africa gained its freedom in 1994 in all its outward manifestations; inwardly, with the exception of a small minority of black and white entrepreneurs, the general population has neither benefitted nor thrived, and moreover has not realised its latent potential, mainly because of the defects in the monetary system. If we are to achieve real freedom, it is imperative that monetary reform be pursued with the same vigour and intensity as was displayed towards political reform during the struggle years. But that requires understanding the complex issues of how money is created, whom it belongs to and whose interests it serves.

In this book, Goodson has not only sketched numerous successes of previous states rather than private banking systems, but has also provided us with a blueprint which may address many of our entrenched social problems, such as low economic growth, high unemployment and declining services.

Albeit decidedly controversial, this is a book which thinking South Africans should read as an inspiration for political action.

In his address before the American Newspaper Publishers Association on 27 Apri, 1961, President John F. Kennedy famously stated: "Without debate, without criticism, no administration and no country can succeed – and no republic can survive. That is why the Athenian lawmaker Solon decreed it a crime for any citizen to shrink from controversy."

Prince Mangosuthu Buthelezi MP
President of the Inkatha Freedom Party
Republic of South Africa

Introduction

History is the most crucial subject of any educational system superseding science and the humanities in importance. Within its fabric, it holds the culture, traditions, beliefs, ethos and *raison d'etre* necessary for the continued existence of any people. If history is compromised by falsifications and omissions, which are frequently imposed by outsiders, then that civilisation will decay and finally collapse, as may be observed in the slow disintegration of Western civilisation since 1945. George Orwell expressed a similar sentiment in '1984' when he wrote: "The most effective way to destroy people is to deny and obliterate their own understanding of history."

Winston Churchill once made the observation that the further one goes back into history, the clearer the picture becomes. By employing this technique the author is hopeful that any doubts, which readers may have concerning his analysis and exegesis of modern historical events will be assuaged, if not entirely eliminated.

For any nation/state/society/community to have full sovereignty and independence in its affairs, absolute control over the means it employs to exchange goods and services must reside with the organs, which represent the people, and must not be delegated to private individuals.

Throughout recorded history periods of state control of the money supply have been synonymous with eras of prosperity, peace, cultural enrichment, full employment and zero inflation. However, when private bankers usurp control of the money creation process, the inevitable results are recurring cycles of prosperity and poverty, unemployment, embedded inflation and

9

an enormous and ever increasing transfer of wealth and political power to this tiny clique, who control this exploitative monetary system. Whenever these private and central bankers have been opposed in the past by nations seeking restoration of an honest money system, these parasitic bankers have invariably invoked a "patriotic" war in order to defeat the much maligned "enemy". This has been a feature of almost all wars during the past 300 plus years.

This book provides insights as to how private bankers since ancient times have abused monetary systems, whether they are based on coin, bank notes, cheque or electronic money, by creating money out of nothing as an interest bearing debt in order to arrogate supreme power to themselves. It also provides a record, both ancient and modern, of societies and civilisations which have flourished in an environment free from the burden of usury.

The solution is simple and self-evident. If we wish to obtain our liberation and sovereignty from the enslavement imposed by the private bankers, we must dismantle their fractional reserve system of banking and supporting central banks, or we ourselves shall be destroyed and consigned to oblivion.

Stephen Mitford Goodson

Chapter I

How Usury Destroyed the Roman Empire

Money, being naturally barren, to make it breed money is preposterous and a perversion from the end of its institution, which was only to serve the purpose of exchange and not of increase... Men called bankers we shall hate, for they enrich themselves while doing nothing. — Aristotle, Politics

The monetary systems of the Roman era (753BC – 565AD) may be divided into three distinct periods, where units of three different metals were used as the means of exchanging goods and services.Although there is evidence of modern human occupation (*Homo sapiens sapiens*) in the Rome area going back 14,000 years (with Neanderthals having lived there approximatley 140,000 years ago), Rome, as a city, is traditionally said to have been founded by Romulus and Remus in 753BC in a region surrounding the Palatine Hills, also known as Latium. According to the legend, Romulus (who killed his brother Remus) became its first king, but later shared the throne with Titus Tatius, the ruler of the Sabines.

Around 600BC Latium came under the control of the Etruscans. This lasted until the last king, Tarquin the Proud, was expelled in 509BC and the Roman Republic was established. The Etruscans, a people of Aryan origin, created one of the most advanced civilisations of that period and built roads, temples and numerous public buildings in Rome.

The first "money" used in Rome was the cow. This was not true money, but a barter system. Many early peoples used cattle as a medium of exchange. According to the legend of Herakles and the Augean stables, the cattle kept there, over 3,000 in number, represented the treasury of King Augeas.

The Copper Age (753 – 267BC)

As time went on, the Romans took to using, instead of cattle, irregular lumps of copper or bronze. These lumps were called *aes rude* (rough metal) and had to be weighed for each transaction.

There was an increase in trade and Rome became one of the most prosperous cities in the ancient world. This prosperity was based on uncoined copper, later bronze, metal which was measured by weight according to a fixed system of units. It was issued by the Roman Treasury in the form of ingots weighing 3½ lbs (1.6kg) with the full backing of the state and was known as *aes signatum* (stamped metal), because it was stamped by the government with a cow, eagle or elephant or other image. Sometimes they were made to resemble a scallop shell. In 289BC these ingots were replaced by discoidal, cast leaded bronze coins *aes grave* (heavy metal). They represented national money and "were paid into circulation by the state and [each was] only of value inasmuch as the symbols on which its numbers were recorded, were scarce or otherwise."[1] This money was thus based on law rather than the metallic content (although that content was standardised, and the coin did have some intrinsic value, unlike most coins today). This can be considered as an early example of the successful use of fiat money.

While fiat money is much criticised in some quarters, for example by the followers of Austrian economist Ludwig von Mises,[2] there is nothing wrong with it, as long as it is issued by government, not by private bankers, and is carefully protected against counterfeiters. Non-fiat money, in contrast, has the serious drawback that whoever sets the prices of gold and silver, i.e. private bankers, can control the nation's economy.

---

1   D. Astle, *The Babylonian Woe*, Private Edition, Toronto 1975, 162. This system bears many similarities to the *pelanors* or ingots of iron, which were used by the Spartans as the basis of their monetary system.

2   Ludwig von Mises (1881-1973) was one of the leaders of the Austrian School of Economics and an ardent proponent of the gold standard.

Roman *Aes Grave*, bronze coins 241-235 BC.

Up to 300BC there was an unsurpassed increase in public and private wealth of the Romans. This may be measured in the gain in land. After the conclusion of the Second Latin War in 338BC and the defeat of the Etruscans, the Roman Republic increased in size from 2,135 square miles (5,525 sq km) to 10,350 square miles (26,805 sq km) or 20% of peninsular Italy. In tandem with the expansion of its land area the population rose from about 750,000 to one million with 150,000 persons living in Rome itself.

A partnership was formed between the Senate and the people known as *Senatus Populusque Romanus* (SPQR, the Senate and People of Rome). The political leaders were renowned for their frugality and honest virtue. The means of exchange was strictly regulated in accordance with the increase in population and trade and there was zero inflation. Debt-bondage *nexum*, whereby a free man offered his services as security for a loan + interest, and where in cases of non-payment the debt had to be worked off, was abolished after Plebian agitation by the *lex Poetelia* [3] in 326BC.

---

3   For an unsparing indictment of the harmful effects of usury on the general population prior to the promulgation of the *lex Poetilia* see Titus Livius, *The History of Rome*, Book II, English translation, William Heinemann Ltd, London, 1919.

The Silver Age (267 – 27BC)

The traditional money system was destroyed in 267BC when the patrician elite obtained the privilege to mint silver coinage. This change was typified by a patrician who went to the Temple of Juno Moneta (from whence the word money is derived), and converted a sack full of silver *denarii* to five times its original value by the simple expedient of stamping a new value on the coins. He thus pocketed a very substantial difference in seigniorage for his own private account.

The early Roman silver coin was known as the *drachma* and was modelled on a coin used in the Greek south of the peninsula. It was later replaced with the smaller and lighter *denarius*. There was also a half *denarius*, called the *quinarius* and a quarter unit called the *sestertius*. Still later the system was supplemented with the *victoriatus*, somewhat lighter than the *denarius* and probably intended to facilitate trade with Rome's Greek neighbours.

There were very few deposits of silver in the Italian peninsula and as a consequence the Roman army had to be expanded, in order to conquer territories to obtain supplies. The Roman peasants, who had provided the Republic with food independence, were drafted in increasing numbers into the army. Agricultural production, especially corn, declined and the peasant farms were replaced by *latifundia*, which were large estates worked by slaves. Wheat also had to be imported from North Africa.

Tensions about granting citizenship and enfranchisement between Rome and her Italic allies resulted in the Social War (90-89BC). This lack of enfranchisement had led to the fragmentation of Roman society and the alienation of the working class citizens, who were treated as chattel and who had no responsibilities and therefore no commitment towards the state. Until as late as the Second Punic War (218-201BC), they were not allowed to serve in the army. This is a classic example of a society which had been monetarised. The Republic was weakened and there

Roman Republican silver *Denarius*
with (left) goddess Juno Moneta and (right) a victorious boxer.

was increasing despotism. Piracy became a major problem, with raids taking place on the coast, villas being sacked and travellers kidnapped. Violence became endemic and gangsters and terrorists were active in Rome, as there was no police force to maintain law and order. These are inevitable consequences of a society in which money has become the highest ethos.

There was also political intrigue amongst the elite. Economic deprivation caused discontent amongst the poor, who were increasingly slaves from North Africa, and social unrest. This turmoil culminated in the revolt led by Spartacus in 73-71BC. (The first and second revolts were in 135-132BC and in 104-100BC).

The Jewish Role in the Collapse

The first known Jews who arrived in Rome in 161BC, were Yehuda and Maccabee. These early Roman Jews employed themselves as craftsmen, peddlers and shopkeepers. In the last occupation they also indulged in money lending. As a community they lived separately in apartments. They governed themselves according to their own laws and were exempt from military service.

Expulsion of the Jews from Rome by Emperor Hadrian 135AD. From a 15th Century manuscript in the Bibliothèque de l'Arsenal in Paris.

In 139BC the Jews, who were not Roman citizens, were expelled by Praetor Hispanus for proselytising, but they soon returned. In 19AD by means of a *senatus consultum* Emperor Tiberius expelled 4,000 Jews, who had been involved in various scandals, but none of these expulsions was properly enforced and their continued presence, in particular as usurers, would play a significant role in the decline and collapse of the Roman Empire.

Julius Caesar. Commissioned in 1696 for the Gardens of Versailles.

Julius Caesar

Julius Caesar (100-44BC) was born into an aristocratic family on July 12, 100BC. He was tall and fair-headed and practised briefly as a lawyer before becoming a brilliant military commander who conquered Gaul (France) in 59-52BC. After his defeat of Pompey the Great in 48BC at Pharsalus, Caesar became the undisputed leader of the Roman Republic. On his return to Italy in September 45BC, Caesar found the streets and cities crowded with homeless people, who had been forced off the land by usurers and land monopolists. 300,000 people had to be fed daily at the public granary. Usury was flourishing with disastrous consequences.[4]

---

4   "The imperial democracy that held the world beneath its sway, from the senators who bore historic names down to the humblest tiller of the soil, from Julius Caesar down to the smallest shopkeeper in the back streets of Rome, was at the mercy of a small group of usurers," as quoted in G. Ferrero, *Greatness and Decline of the Roman Empire*, Vol. vi,

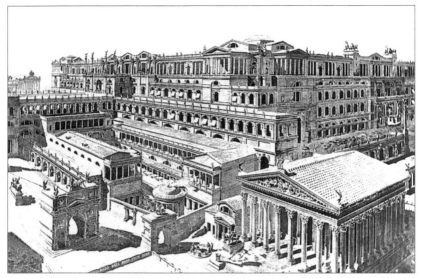

The Forum Romanum was commissioned by Julius Caesar in 54BC and dedicated by him in 46BC. It was the very centre of ancient Rome where Caesar would meet his untimely end on March 15, 44BC.

The principal usurers, many of whom were Jewish,[5] were charging interest rates as high as 48% per annum. As Lucius Annaeus Seneca (4BC-65AD), the philosopher, would later remark in *de Superstitione* "The customs of that most criminal nation have gained such strength that they have now been received in all lands. The conquered have given laws to the conqueror."

At that time there were two main political parties: the *Optimates* centered around the nobility, the Senate and the privileged few; and the *Populares*, who represented the citizens. Caesar immediately assumed leadership of the latter.

William Heinemann Ltd, London, 1908, 223.

5   Cicero, Marcus Tullius: "Softly! Softly! I want none but the judges to hear me. The Jews have already gotten me into a fine mess, as they have many another gentleman. I have no desire to furnish further grist for their mills," as quoted in W. Grimstad, *Antizion*, Noontide Press, Torrance, California, 1985, 29. Cicero was serving as defence counsel at the trial of one Flaccus, a Roman official, who interfered with Jewish gold shipments to their international headquarters (then, as now) in Jerusalem. Cicero himself was not a nobody, and for one of his stature to have to "speak softly" shows that he was in the presence of a dangerously powerful sphere of influence. In which case, one wonders who the real persecutors were.

Caesar fully understood the evils of usury and how to counter them. "He recognized the profound truth that money is a national agent, created by law for a national purpose, and that no classes of men should withhold it from circulation so as to cause panics, in order that speculators could advance the rates of interest, or could buy up property at ruinous prices after such panic."[6]

Caesar introduced the following social reforms:

1. Restoration of property was done at the much lower valuations which held prior to the civil war. (49-45BC).
2. Several remissions of rents were granted.
3. Large numbers of poor citizens and discharged veterans were settled on allotments.
4. Free housing was provided to 80,000 impoverished families.
5. Soldiers' pay was increased from 123 to 225 *denarii*.
6. The corn dole was regulated.
7. Provincial communities were enfranchised.
8. Confusion in the calendar was removed by fixing it at 365¼ days from 1 January 44BC.

His monetary reforms were as follows:

1. State debt levels were immediately reduced by 25%.
2. Control of the mint was transferred from the patricians (usurers) to government.
3. Cheap metal coins were issued as the means of exchange.
4. It was ruled that interest could not be levied at more than 1% per month.
5. It was decreed that interest could not be charged on interest and that the total interest charged could never exceed the capital loaned (*in duplum* rule).
6. Slavery was abolished as a means of settling debt.
7. Aristocrats were forced to employ their capital and not hoard it.

---

6   T.E. Watson, *Sketches from Roman History*, The Barnes Review, Washington, DC, 2011, (first published in 1908), 84-85.

Gold coin minted by Emperor Alexander Severus 222-235AD.

These measures enraged the aristocrats and plutocrats whose "livelihood" was now severely restricted. They therefore conspired to murder Caesar, the hero of the people. On that fateful morning of 15 March 44BC, only four years after assuming power he arrived at the Senate building unarmed, having dismissed his military guard, who had previously been in constant attendance. Surrounded by 60 conspirators he was stabbed to death and received 23 wounds.

The Gold Age (27BC – 476AD)

In 27BC shortly after Caesar's death (and his deification) the Romans adopted the gold standard, which would have far reaching implications for the financial stability of the empire and lead directly to its demise. Previously, during the days of the Roman Republic, gold coins were issued only in times of great need, such as during the Second Punic War or the campaign of Lucius Cornelius Sulla. There were few gold mines in Europe, except in remote places like Wales, Transylvania and Spain and therefore most of the supplies could only be secured from the east. This in turn required a large and expensive army, which became engaged in constant conflict at the empire's fringes.

The gold coin was known as an *aureus*. Also in circulation were the silver *denarius* and various copper coins: the *sestertius*, *dupondius* and the *as*.

The scarcity of gold or commodity money frequently induced periods of deflation as a result of the lack of a circulating means of exchange. In 13BC a measure of relief was provided when the weight of the gold *aureus* was reduced from 122 to 72 grains and this remained the standard weight until 310AD. However, metals continued to flow eastwards in order to pay for luxury items, religious dues and usury payments. Furthermore wear and tear resulted in the loss of one third of total coinage in circulation over a 100 year period.

As gold was treated as a commodity, its debasement was not tolerated. Emperor Constantine (275-337AD) personally ordered death for counterfeiting, and the burning of public minters who committed falsification. Money changers, who did not report a counterfeit gold bezant (*solidus*), were immediately flogged, enslaved and exiled. These regulations were effective for the bezant, which weighed 70 grains and was slightly more than the bezant that was still circulating in 1025AD and weighed 68 grains.

In 313AD Christianity was tolerated by the Edict of Milan and from 380AD was established as the official religion by Emperor Theodosius I (347-395AD). From this time monetary power resided in the religious authority of the *pontifex maximus*. A feature of the imperial era was social injustice and the undermining of the middle classes through excessive taxation. The Roman businessman was not a trader, but a looter of the provinces, as the homeland had a weak industrial production base, which was incapable of providing the required manufactured goods. As the monetarisation of society continued, with the rich parasitising of the common man, the plebians became more like slaves. The abolition of the jury system was symptomatic of the declining respect and importance for the common man in Roman society.

Role of the Church in the Decline and Fall

The tax that Emperor Constantine decreed, viz. that 1/10 of all income had to be tithed to the Christian church, hastened the destruction of the empire. Eventually the Church held one third to one half of all lands and accumulated wealth. This concentration of wealth produced a great scarcity of coinage. Money existed, but there was no circulation or distribution of goods and services. Instead of recycling the tithed money by means of investment in the community or charitable works such as construction of hospitals, schools and libraries, vast hoards of gold were concentrated behind the 20 foot (6.1m) thick walls of the fortress city of Constantinople and the Vatican fortress in Rome.

In its last years in the fifth and sixth centuries the Roman Empire had become a parasitic organism, subject to alternating phases of inflation and deflation. Its economic ruination preceded its political ruination. There was no industrial production, almost all food had to be imported and usury was practised on an unprecedented scale. The wealth of the empire that was not held by the Church, was controlled by 2,000 Roman families. The rest of the population lived in poverty.

Consequences

The implosion of the western half of the empire in 476AD, after repeated military incursions by the Goths and Vandals, resulted in the Dark Ages. A punishing multi-century deflationary depression followed. According to the United States Silver Commission of 1876 the metallic money of the Roman Empire at its height amounted to $1.8 billion, but by the end of the Dark Ages it had shrunk to $200 million. Agriculture was reduced to subsistence level. Large sailing vessels vanished as there was no trade. Commerce stagnated. Arts and science were lost and the knowledge of cement-making disappeared.

Major factors in the decline of the Roman Empire were the concentration of wealth,[7] the absence of mining deposits for

---

7   "When the Government of old Egypt fell, 4 per cent of all the people owned all the wealth. When the Babylonian civilisation toppled, 3 per cent of the people owned all the wealth. When old Persia went down to destruction, 2 per cent of the people owned all the wealth. When ancient Greece fell in ruins, one-half of 1 per cent of the people owned all the wealth. When the Roman Empire fell, two thousand people owned the

industrial production, and the vast importation of non-White slaves with the resultant degradation of the genetic value of the nation. By the 4th century AD, as a result of the continuing decline in Roman female fertility, slaves outnumbered citizens by five to one. The most important economic reason was an inadequate supply of an inexpensive circulating medium of money and the false notion that money should be a commodity. Thus from an economic perspective, the lessons from the fall of Rome are that a dishonest economic system will inevitably contribute to the forces of dissolution. No society can survive a false economic system. For any society to function and prosper it is absolutely fundamental that the means of exchange be issued free of debt and interest by the legal authority of the state as representatives of the people in perpetuity.

wealth of the civilized world. Then followed the Dark Ages, from which the world did not recover until wealth was no longer concentrated. Today less than 1 per cent of the people controls 90 per cent of the wealth of these United States." – as quoted in R. Maguire, "Money Made Mysterious", *American Mercury* magazine, New York, 1958, 98. (*American Mercury* was founded by H.L. Mencken in 1924).

Chapter II

The Hidden Origins of the Bank of England

...all great events have been distorted, most of the important causes concealed...If the history of England is ever written by one who has the knowledge and the courage, the world would be astonished.
- Benjamin Disraeli, Prime Minister of Great Britain

Ancient England

King Offa ruled the Kingdom of Mercia,[1] which was bounded by the rivers Trent and Mersey in the north, the Thames Valley in the south, Wales in the west and East Anglia and Essex in the east from 757 to 791 AD. It was one of the seven autonomous kingdoms of the Anglo-Saxon Heptarchy.

Offa was a wise and able administrator and a kind-hearted leader. He established the first monetary system in England. On account of the scarcity of gold he used silver for coinage and as a store of wealth. The standard unit of exchange was a pound of silver divided into 240 pennies. The pennies were stamped with a star (Old English *stearra*), from which the word sterling is derived. In 787 King Offa introduced a statute prohibiting usury, viz. the charging of interest on money lent, a concept which dates back to the pagan era. The laws against usury were further entrenched by King Alfred (865-99), who directed that the property of usurers be forfeited, while in 1050 Edward the Confessor (1042-66) decreed not only forfeiture, but that a usurer be declared an outlaw and be banished for life.

---

1   Latinisation of Mierce.

First Jewish Migration and Expulsion

The Jews first arrived in England in 1066 in the wake of William I's defeat of King Harold II at Hastings on 14 October. These Jews came from Rouen, 75 miles (121 km) from Falaise in Normandy, where William the Conqueror was born illegitimately as William the Bastard. Although the historical record does not indicate whether they promoted the idea of a military invasion of England, these Jews had at the very least financed it. For this support they were richly rewarded by being allowed to practise usury under royal protection.[2]

The consequences for the English people were disastrous. By charging rates of interest of 33% per annum on lands mortgaged by nobles and 300% per annum on tools of trade or chattels pledged by workmen, within two generations one quarter of all English lands were in the hands of Jewish usurers. At his death in 1186, Aaron of Lincoln was declared to be the richest man in England and it was estimated that his wealth exceeded that of King Henry II.[3] Furthermore the Jewish immigrants undermined the ethos of the guilds and exasperated the English merchants by selling a large variety of goods under one roof. They also played a prominent role in the clipping of silver coins and the melting of them into bullion and the plating of tin with silver.

The famous economist, Dr. William Cunningham, compares "the activity of the Jews in England from the eleventh century onward to a sponge, which sucks up all the wealth of the land and thereby hinders all economic development. Interesting too, is the proof that even at this early period the government did everything in its power to make the Jews take up decent trades and honest work and thereby at the same time amalgamate with the rest of the population, but all to no purpose."[4]

---

2   S.M. Goodson, In Praise of Medieval England, *Spearhead*, July 2005.

3   R. Chazan, *The Jews of Medieval Western Christendom 1000-1500*, Cambridge University Press, New York, 2006, 159.

4   W. Cunningham, *The Growth of English Industry and Commerce during the Early and*

By the beginning of the 13th century many nobles were in danger of losing their lands through usury and taxation. In 1207 an enormous sum of £60,000 was levied in taxes on the Christian population. The Jews also paid tax, but at a lower rate and on grossly understated income and wealth.[5] Nobles who borrowed from Jewish moneylenders and from the King and his agents had to have their mortgages registered on the Treasury Rolls. As soon as a noble got into financial difficulty, the King would buy the debt from the moneylender and seize the land for himself. King John (1199-1216) was "utterly reckless" in pursuit of this depraved and dishonest policy, and was moreover "profligate, incompetent and utterly beholden to his Jews."[6]

In 1215 the nobles revolted and forced King John to sign the Magna Carta on 15 June 1215. This document consists of 61 clauses relating to the establishment of various constitutional and legal rights, but its principal purpose was to cancel the bonds of the Jewish moneylenders and to abolish usury and the privileged position of the Jews. On 19 October 1216 King John died and was succeeded by his nine year old son Henry III, who ruled from 1219 to 1272. His reign was little better than that of his father and 19 of the clauses affecting the Jews were abrogated the following year. However, his heir Edward I (1272-1307) soon realised that Jews had no place in English society[7] and that if he did not take action,

---

Middle Ages, Cambridge University Press, 3rd edition, 1896, 201.

5   Background to the Magna Carta, *The Occidental Observer*, May 19, 2013.

6   *Ibid.*

7   The ritual murder of pre-adolescent Christian boys was the tipping point, which resulted in the expulsion of the Jews. At the time of the Jewish Passover a boy would be captured and then bled to death. The blood would then be mixed with unleavened dough, baked and later eaten as a rabbinical cake. The first known case occurred in 1144 and the most famous one is that of Little St Hugh of Lincoln in 1255. King Henry III personally ordered a judicial investigation, which included a forensic examination by the judges. 91 Jews were arrested for their participation in this gruesome murder, in which the victim was tortured, crucified, bled to death and then dumped into a well. Details of this court case may be found in the Close Rolls of the Realm and the Patent Rolls, Henry III at The National Archives, Kew, Richmond, Surrey, TW9 4DU. Geoffrey Chaucer wrote a poem commemorating Little Hugh's murder in the Prioress's Tale, which forms part of the *Canterbury Tales*. The Brothers Grimm wrote *"Der Judenstein"* (The Jew's Stone) about the ritual murder of two year old Andreas (Anderl) Oxner in Rinn, Austria in 1492. *In My Irrelevant Defence:*

The barons, including the author's ancestor Roger Bertram, Lord of Mitford, forced King John to sign the Magna Carta in Runnymede on 15 June 1215.

he would be in danger of losing his throne. In 1233 and 1275 Statutes of Jewry were passed which abolished all forms of usury. As many of these Jews could no longer earn a "living", a statute was passed by King Edward on 18 July 1290 compelling the entire Jewish population of 16,511 to leave England forever;[8] one of over 100 hundred expulsions which have been recorded throughout European history. The announcement was greeted with great joy and jubilation throughout the land. Unlike the modern practice of ethnic cleansing, the Jews, after paying a tax of 1/15 of the value of their movables and 1/10 of their specie, were permitted to leave with all their goods and chattels. Any Jew who remained after 1 November 1290 (All Saints Day) was liable to be executed.

Meditations Inside Gaol and Out on Jewish Ritual Murder, The I.F.L. Printing and Publishing Co., London, 1938, 57 pp. Arnold Leese alleges that ritual murder was still taking place in the 20th century. In February 2007, Israeli Professor Ariel Toaff, son of Elio Toaff the former Chief Rabbi of Rome, wrote *Pasque di sangue: Ebrei d'Europa e omicidi rituali* (Passovers of Blood: The Jews of Europe and Ritual Murders) in which he confirms the prevalence of ritual murder in medieval Italy. For an analysis of this work see *The Bloody Passovers of Dr Toaff* by Israel Shamir www.israelshamir.net/English/Eng11.htm

8   D. Astle, *The Tallies, A Tangled Tale and The Beginning and the Ending*, Private Edition, Toronto, 1997, 40 & 43. Astle is of the opinion that some of these Jews settled in Switzerland and established the original three cantons of Uri, Schwyz and Ob - and Niwalden one year later.

The Glorious Middle Ages

With the banishment of the moneylenders and the abolition of usury,[9] taxes were moderate and there was no state debt, as the interest-free tally stick[10] was used for government expenditures. This ancient instrument of finance known to the Saracens and possibly also to the Chinese is derived from the Latin word *tallia* meaning a stick. A tally stick was made out of hazel, willow or boxwood because these woods split easily. They were usually eight inches in length (20.3cm) (from forefinger to thumb) and half an inch (1.3cm) wide, although they could be up to eight feet (2.44m) long. The denominations were indicated by different sized cuts in the wood. £1,000 were marked by cutting out the thickness of the palm of a hand, £100 by the breadth of the little finger, £1 that of a swelling barleycorn, shillings somewhat less and pence were marked by incisions. The payee was recorded on the flat sides. When all the details had been recorded on the tally it was split nearly to the bottom, so that one part retained a stump or handle on which a hole would be bored. This was known as the counter tally or counterfoil and was held on a rod at the Exchequer. The flat strip (without the stump) was given to the payee. As no two pieces of wood are identical, it was impossible to forge a tally stick.

Tally sticks were first introduced during the reign of King Henry II (1100-35) and would remain in circulation until 1783.[11] It was, however, during the period 1290-1485 that tallies would reach their apogee and constitute the principal means of state finance. Tallies were used not only to pay state salaries, but to finance major items of infrastructure such as construction of the

---

9   In 1364 Edward III empowered the City of London to issue an *Ordinatio contra Usurarios* and a further Act was passed in 1390.

10   D. Astle, *op.cit.*, 12-17.

11   In an act of supreme irony on 16 October, 1834 piles of broken tally sticks were used to heat the House of Commons. The fiercely burning tally sticks raged out of control and the entire complex, with the exception of Westminster Hall and St Stephen's Cloister, was burnt to the ground. The mosaic floor of the entrance hall of the rebuilt House of Commons (possibly as a result of Rothschild influence) was designed in the shape of a giant Star of David.

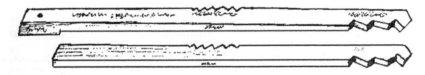

Medieval tally sticks from the 15th century.

wall of the city of London, public buildings and ports. The exact amount of tallies in circulation is not known, but as late as 1694 £17 million worth were still in existence. This was a prodigious sum as the King's annual budget rarely exceeded £2.5 million and a labourer earned a penny a day.

With tolerable taxes,[12] no state debt and no interest to pay, England enjoyed a period of unparalleled growth and prosperity. The average labourer worked only 14 weeks and enjoyed 160 to 180 holidays. According to Lord William Leverhulme,[13] a writer of that time, "The men of the 15th century were very well paid", in fact so well paid that the purchasing power of their wages and their standard of living would only be exceeded in the late 19th century. A labourer could provide for all the necessities his family required. They were well clothed in good woollen cloth and had plenty of meat and bread.

Houston Stewart Chamberlain, the Anglo-German philosopher, confirms these living conditions in his *The Foundations of the XIXth Century*.

"In the thirteenth century, when the Teutonic races began to build their new world, the agriculturalist over nearly the whole of Europe was a freer man, with a more assured existence,

---

12 G.M. Trevelyan, *English Social History, A Survey of Six Centuries Chaucer to Queen Victoria*, Longmans Green and Co., London, 1948 writes that England was "a land whose people would not endure taxation" 63 and that "an obstinate refusal to pay taxes was a characteristic of the English at this period," 107.

13 R.K. Hoskins, *War Cycles – Peace Cycles*, The Virginian Publishing Company, Lynchburg, Virginia, 1985, 54.

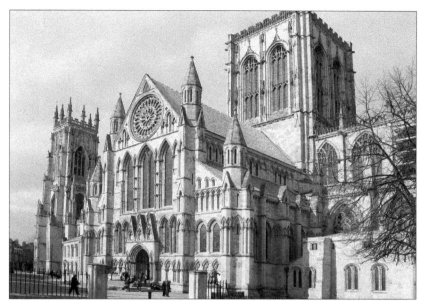

With the average labourer required to work only 14 weeks in a year, many voluntarily gave of their time to build England's magnificent cathedrals. The York Minster was completed in 1472 and has the largest expanse of stained glass in the world.

than he is today; copyhold[14] was the rule, so that England, for example – today a seat of landlordism – was even in the fifteenth century almost entirely in the hands of thousands of farmers, who were not only legal owners of their land, but possessed in addition far-reaching free rights to common pastures and woodlands."[15]

During their spare hours many craftsmen volunteered their skills in building some of England's magnificent cathedrals, which reinforces one of the basic tenets of Western civilisation that without leisure time, the fostering of culture is not possible. George Macauley Trevelyan, the English social historian, describes these accomplishments as follows:

---

14 Copyhold was a form of manorial land rights which evolved from the system of serfdom.

15 H.S. Chamberlain, *The Foundations of the Nineteenth Century*, The Bodley Head, London, 1912, Vol. II, 354-355.

15th Century Merrie England - Celebrating the 1st
of May dancing around the maypole.

"The continuous but ever-moving tradition of ecclesiastical
architecture still proceeded on its majestic way, filling England
with towering forests of masonry of which the beauty and
grandeur have never been rivaled either by the Ancients or
the Moderns...In the newer churches the light no longer
crept but flooded in, through the stained glass, of which the
secret is today even more completely lost than the magic of
the architecture."[16]

Although King Henry VIII (1509-47) relaxed the laws regarding
usury in 1509, they were subsequently repealed by his son King
Edward VI (1547-53) by an Act of 1552 whose preamble stated
that "usury is by word of God, utterly prohibited, as a vice most
odious and detestable..."

---

16   G.M. Trevelyan, *op.cit.*, 51.

End of a Golden Era

During the 17th century this golden era came to a tragic end. Large numbers of Jews, who had been expelled from Spain in 1492 by Isabella I of Castile and Ferdinand II of Aragon[17] on account of their persistent involvement in usury and unethical business practices, had settled in Holland. Although the Dutch were at that time an important maritime power, the Jewish usurers based in Amsterdam desired to return to England, where their prospects for expanding the operations of their money-lending empire were far more promising.

During the reign of Queen Elizabeth I (1558-1603) small numbers of Marranos-Spanish Jews, who had converted to a sham form of Christianity, settled in London. Many of them practised as goldsmiths, accepting deposits of gold for safekeeping, and then issuing ten times the amount of gold received as gold receipts, that is loans with interest. These receipts, a forerunner of the fraudulent fractional reserve system of banking, were initially lent to the Crown or Treasury at 8% per annum, but according to Samuel Pepys,[18] the diarist and Secretary to the Admiralty, the interest rate increased to as much as 20% and even 30 % per annum.[19] The rate of interest merchants paid often exceeded 33% per annum, even though the legal rate was only 6% per annum.[20] Workmen and poor people bore the brunt of these extortionate rates of interest by having to pay 60%, 70% or even 80% per annum.[21] According to Michael Godfrey, the author of a pamphlet entitled *A Short Account of the Bank of England*, two to three million pounds had been lost through the bankruptcies of goldsmiths and the disappearance of their clerks.[22]

---

17   Alhambra Decree also known as the Edict of Expulsion.

18   A. M. Andreadēs, *History of the Bank of England*, P.S. King & Son Ltd, London, 1935, 35. Pepys described these extortionate rates of interest as "a most horrid shame."

19   *Ibid.*, 24. The author has also relied on Israel Disraeli's *"Usurers of the Seventeenth Century."* www.gutenberg.org/ebooks/16350?msg=welcome_stranger

20   *Ibid.*, 24.

21   *Ibid.*, 47.

22   *Ibid.*, 24-25.

Cromwell and the English Civil War

In 1534, by the Act of Supremacy, the Church of England was established as the official religion of England by King Henry VIII. During the 16th and 17th centuries Puritan beliefs based on the teachings of John Wycliffe and John Calvin[23] gained an increasing number of adherents. The Puritans considered the Bible to be the true law of God and emphasised Bible reading, prayer and preaching and the simplification of the ritual of the sacraments.

The Stuart King Charles I (1625-49), who wished to maintain the pre-eminence of the Anglican Church, came into intensified conflict with the Puritans, who were making great progress in proselytising the population. After the assassination of Charles's trusted friend and adviser, the Duke of Buckingham in 1628, he gradually became more isolated. The growing religious division provided a perfect opportunity for exploitation by the Jewish conspirators. As Israel D'Israeli, the father of prime minister Benjamin D'Israeli, wrote in *The Life and Reign of Charles I*, "The nation was artfully divided into Sabbatarians and Sabbath Breakers."[24]

In 1640 one of the leaders of the clandestine Jewish community Fernandez Carvajal, a merchant and spy, who was also known as "the Great Jew", organised an armed militia of about 10,000 operatives, who were used to intimidate the people of London and sow confusion. Large numbers of pamphlets and leaflets were also distributed.[25]

Civil war soon followed between the Royalists (Anglicans) and Roundheads (Puritans) and lasted from 1642-48. The Roundheads with their 'New Model Army' were victorious and an estimated 190,000 persons or 3.8% of the population died.

---

23 A.H.M. Ramsay, *The Nameless War*, Britons Publishing Co., London, 1952, 11. Calvin originally came from France where his name was spelt Cauin, a corruption of Cohen. At a B'nai Brith meeting in Paris reported in *The Catholic Gazette* of February 1936 he was claimed to have been of Jewish extraction.

24 *Ibid.*, 11.

25 *Ibid.*, 12-13.

A pamphlet of the late 1650s portrays Oliver Cromwell as
the monarch of England.

The leader of the Roundheads was Oliver Cromwell (1599-
1658), whose 'New Model Army' was not only outfitted and
provisioned by the chief contractor and professional agitator,
Fernandez Carvajal, but also bankrolled by Jewish moneylenders
in Amsterdam. The leader of the Dutch Jews, Manasseh Ben
Israel,[26] sent begging petitions to Cromwell asking that the Jews
be allowed to immigrate to England in return for the financial
favours, which he had so generously arranged.[27]

The Regicide of King Charles I

The treachery to which Cromwell descended is revealed in
correspondence between himself and the Synagogue of Mulheim,
Germany.

---

26   *Ibid.*, 13.
27   A. M. Andreadēs, *op.cit.*, 30.

16 June 1647

From O.C. (Oliver Cromwell) to Ebenezer Pratt

"In return for financial support will advocate admission of Jews to England: This however impossible while Charles living. Charles cannot be executed without trial, adequate grounds for which do not at present exist. Therefore advise that Charles be assassinated, but will have nothing to do with arrangements for procuring an assassin, though willing to help in his escape."

In reply was dispatched the following:-

12 July 1647

To O.C. from Ebenezer Pratt

"Will grant financial aid as soon as Charles removed and Jews admitted. Assassination too dangerous. Charles shall be given an opportunity to escape: His recapture will make trial and execution possible. The support will be liberal, but useless to discuss terms until trial commences." [28]

King Charles was staying as a virtual prisoner in Holmby House, Northamptonshire. On 4 June 1647 500 revolutionaries seized the King, but then allowed him to escape to the Isle of Wight where he was subsequently arrested. On 5 December 1648 the House of Commons decided "That the King's concessions were satisfactory to a settlement."[29]

---

28 A.H.M. Ramsay, op. cit., 14-15. According to a letter published in *Plain English* on 3 September, 1921:- "The Learned Elders have been in existence for a much longer period than they have perhaps suspected. My friend, Mr. L.D. van Valckert of Amsterdam, has recently sent me a letter containing two extracts from the Synagogue at Mulheim. The volume in which they are contained was lost at some period during the Napoléonic Wars, and has recently come into Mr. van Valckert's possession. It is written in German, and contains extracts of letters sent and received by the authorities of the Mulheim Synagogue."

29 *Ibid.*, 16.

The Execution of King Charles I from a contemporary engraving.

Cromwell then purged the House of Commons with the assistance of Colonel Pryde until there was only a "Rump" of 50 members left, who then duly voted that the King be put on trial. Not a single English lawyer was prepared to draw up a charge sheet against the King. Eventually it was provided by a Dutch Jew, Isaac Dorislaus. The King was forced to participate in a show trial in a High Court of Justice in which two thirds of its members were Levellers[30] from the army. Charles refused to plead, but was found guilty and executed on 30 January 1649. As the procession approached the scaffold large numbers of the crowd shouted "God Save the King!" After the deed had been done there was an enormous groan of anguish.

Second Jewish Migration

From 7-18 December 1655 Cromwell, who was called The Protector held a conference in Whitehall, London, in order to obtain approval for the large-scale immigration of Jews. In spite of the conference being packed with Cromwell's supporters, the overwhelming consensus of the delegates, who were mainly

---

30   An informal alliance of agitators and pamphleteers, who predated the Jacobins and Bolsheviks.

priests, lawyers and merchants, was that the Jews should not be permitted to enter England.[31]

In October 1656 the first Jews were surreptitiously allowed to land freely in England, in spite of strong protests having been lodged by the sub-committee of the Council of State, who declared that these Jews "would be a grave menace to the state and the Christian religion".[32] "…The merchants, without exception, spoke against the admission of the Jews. They declared that the proposed immigrants would be morally harmful to the State, and that their admission would enrich foreigners at the expense of the English."[33]

Cromwell died on 3 September 1658 and was succeeded by his son, Richard who ruled for nine months. Charles I's son Charles II (1660-85) succeeded his executed father. Although he would be the last English monarch to issue money (bank notes) in his own right, he made two fatal errors of governance.

On 1 August 1663 he passed the euphemistically sounding Act for the Encouragement of Trade, which enabled the "export of all foreign coins or bullion of gold or silver, free of interdict, regulation or duties of any kind."[34] During the debate on the bill the Earl of Anglesey presciently observed that "It is dangerous to the peace of the kingdom when it shall be in the power of half-a-dozen or half-a-score of rich, discontented, or factious persons to make a bank (an accumulation) of our own coin and bullion beyond the seas and leave us in want of money when it shall not (no longer) be in the king's power to prevent it."[35]

---

31 H.S.A. Henriques, The Jews and the English Law IV, *The Jewish Quarterly Review*, Vol. 14, No. 4, Jul. 1902, 653-697.

32 A.H.M. Ramsay, *op.cit.*, 16-17.

33 A.M. Hyamson, *A History of the Jews in England*, Methuen, 1928 as quoted in A.N. Field, *All These Things*, Omni Publications, Hawthorne, California, 1936, 215.

34 D. Astle, *op.cit.*, 44.

35 A. Del Mar, *The History of Money in America From the Earliest Times to the Establishment of the Constitution*, Omni Publications, Hawthorne, California, 1966, (first published in 1899), 66.

TO THE
Parliament, The Supream Court of
ENGLAND,

And to the ***Right Honourable*** *the Coun-*
cell of State, Menaſſeh Ben Iſrael, *prayes*
God to give Health, and all Happineſſe :

T is not one cauſe alone (moſt renowned Fathers) which uſeth to move thoſe, who deſire
by their Meditations to benefit Mankind, and
to make them come forth in publique, to de-
dicate their Books to great Men ; for ſome,
and thoſe the moſt, are incited by Covetouſneſſe, that
they may get money by ſo doing, or ſome peece of
Plate of gold, or Silver ; ſometimes alſo that they may
obtaine their Votes, and ſuffrages to get ſome place for
themſelves, or their friends.   But ſome are moved thereto
by meere and pure friendſhip, that ſo they may publick-
ly teſtifie that love and affection, which they bear them,
whoſe names they prefixe to their Books ; let the one, and
the other, pleaſe themſelves, according as they delight in
the reaſon of the Dedication, whether it be good or bad ;
for my part, I beſt like them, who do it upon this ground,
that they may not commend themſelves, or theirs, but
what is for publick good.
    As for me (moſt renowned Fathers) in my dedicating

A 2   this

(3)

Pamphlet published by Menasseh Ben Israel to promote the
re-admission of the Jews to England.

Three years later by means of An Act for the Encouragement of Coinage he permitted private persons i.e. bankers and goldsmiths to mint the coins of the realm at the Royal Mint and thereby acquire the considerable benefits of the seigniorage (the difference between the face value of coins and their production costs) income for their own private account. Furthermore it enabled them to increase or diminish the supply of money in circulation and to raise or lower prices at will to the great detriment of the general population.

His brother James II's (1685-88) reign only lasted three years. He was a victim of unscrupulous pamphleteering and propaganda, which emanated mainly from Holland. A military expedition undertaken by Prince William of Orange eventually dethroned him. Although James's army was numerically superior, he was discouraged from attacking after John Churchill, first Duke of Marlborough suddenly deserted him. According to the *Jewish Encyclopedia*, Churchill subsequently received an annual stipend of £6,000 from the Dutch Jew Solomon de Medina in payment for his treasonous conduct.[36] These vast sums of "blood money" enabled Churchill to proceed with the construction of Blenheim Palace, which was completed at his death in 1722.

William of Orange's military campaign, like that of the other William the Conqueror in 1066, was financed by Jewish bankers. In return for their support William III (1689-1702) would surrender the royal prerogative of issuing England's money free of debt and interest, to a consortium known as The Governor and Company of the Bank of England. A.N. Field in *All these Things* summarises these epochal events known as the Glorious Revolution of 1688, but which was in effect the Infamous Revolution, as follows:

"Thirty-three years after Cromwell had let the Jews into Britain a Dutch Prince arrived from Amsterdam surrounded by a whole swarm of Jews from that financial centre. Driving

---

36   A.H.M. Ramsay, *op.cit.,* 18.

his royal father-in-law [James II] out of the kingdom he graciously consented to ascend the throne of Britain. A very natural result following on this event was the inauguration of the National Debt by the establishment six years later of the Bank of England for the purpose of lending money to the Crown. Britain had paid her way as she went until the Jews arrived. The pawnshop was then opened, and the resulting situation in which the nation finds itself today could not be better described than in the words put by Shakespeare with prophetic vision in the mouth of the dying John of Gaunt:

This land of such dear souls, this dear dear land,
Dear for her reputation through the world,
Is now leased out, I die pronouncing it,
Like to a tenement or pelting farm:
England, bound in with the triumphant sea
Whose rocky shore beats back the envious siege
Of watery Neptune, is now bound in with shame,
With inky blots and rotten parchment bonds:
That England, that was wont to conquer others,
Hath made a shameful conquest of itself.

- Richard II Act II Scene 1

"The history of the second Jewish settlement in Britain is one long trail of parchment bonds shackling the nation in debt. Every step in the ascent of the Jew in the nation's affairs has been marked by the increase and multiplication of debt."[37]

Establishment of the Bank of England

The need for a privately owned central bank was fronted by a retired pirate,[38] William Paterson, when he wrote a pamphlet in 1693 entitled *A Brief Account of the Intended Bank of England.*[39]

---

37   A.N. Field, *op.cit.,* 218.

38   A. M. Andreadēs, *op.cit.,* 60. At that time the profession of buccaneer was not deemed to be disreputable.

39   *Ibid.,* 66.

He would later boast that this Bank "hath the benefit of interest on all moneys which it creates out of nothing."[40] On Thursday, 21 June 1694 subscription lists for the Bank, which had a capital of £1,200,000 were opened. By the following Monday this amount had been fully subscribed.

The ostensible purpose of the bank was to lend King William unlimited sums at 8% per annum to enable the prosecution of war, and in particular the conflict against Louis XIV of France whose country was not on the usury system.[41] The Bank would thus receive from the Crown interest of £100,000 per annum, the additional £4,000 being an administrative fee. The Bank also acquired the right to issue £1,200,000 in bank notes without any gold cover.

Prior to its listing, the byelaws of the Bank were carefully scrutinised by Serjeant-at-Law Creswell Levinz in order to ensure that the Bank complied with its hidden purpose, viz. to fleece the English people in perpetuity by allowing the creation of the nation's money and means of exchange out of nothing at interest. All this fake money was to be accompanied by compounding interest. Levinz was a crypto-Jew or Marrano who practised as an advocate[42] and later served as a judge.

There was much opposition to the establishment of the Bank. Foremost were the goldsmiths and moneylenders, who correctly foresaw that it would bring an end to their usurious racket of fractional reserve banking based on their gold receipts. Landowners and country gentry feared an escalation in interest rates, as the Bank would control the nation's money supply. There were allegations that the Bank would favour certain merchants with low rates of interest. The biggest fear was that "the Bank would grow too powerful and would become the keystone of

40   W.G. Simpson, *Which Way Western Man?*, Yeoman Press, Cooperstown, New York, 1978, 621.

41   F.J. Irsigler, *On The Seventh Day They Created Inflation*, Wynberg, Cape, South Africa, 1980, 5.

42   J.E.T. Rogers, *The First Nine Years of The Bank of England*, Clarendon Press, Oxford, 1887, 4.

Formation of the Bank of England passed by an Act of Parliament
described as "An Act for granting to theire Majesties severall
Rates and Duties upon Tunnage of Shipps and Vessells..."

the commercial world."[43] Unfortunately, this is exactly what
happened, as the Bank of England became the model on which
all subsequent central banks were replicated.

At that time the House of Commons had 514 members consisting
of 243 Tories, 241 Whigs and 28 members whose allegiance was
unknown.[44] About two-thirds of the members were country
gentlemen and it is believed that of the 514 members approximately
20% were illiterate. The bill was debated in July 1694, the high
point in summer, when most of the rural members were engaged
in summer pursuits and the harvesting of their crops.[45] On that
fateful Friday, 27 July 1694 when the Charter of Incorporation
was granted only 42 members were present, all of them Whigs,
as the Tories opposed the bill, who all voted in favour of it. (This
begs the question as to what a quorum consisted of in those days).

---

43 A. M. Andreadēs, *op.cit.*, 69.

44 House of Commons Information Office, House of Commons, London.

45 Legislation for the privately-owned US Federal Reserve Bank was voted on 23
    December 1913, after President Woodrow Wilson had threatened to deny the
    legislators their Christmas recess if they did not vote for the bill. H.S. Kenan, *The
    Federal Reserve Bank*, The Noontide Press, Los Angeles, 1966, 19-20.

Dividend day at the Bank of England. Wood engraved print, circa 1800.

The title of the bill made no mention of the proposed Bank of England, which is only described or one might say secreted, two-thirds down in the unintelligible verbiage - to the layman that is - of the bill.

The opening sentence of the bill reads as follows: "William and Mary by the grace of God, King and Queen of England, Scotland, France and Ireland, defenders of the faith etc. To all for whom these presents shall come greeting." The third sentence, which contains 242 words starts "Whereas in and by a certain Act lately made in Parliament entitled an Act for granting to Their Majesties several rates and duties upon TONNAGE OF SHIPS AND VESSELS, and upon beer, ale, and other liquors, for securing certain recompenses and advantages in the said Act mentioned, to such persons as shall voluntarily advance the sum of fifteen hundred thousand pounds towards carrying on the war with France it is amongst other things enacted......"[46]

---

46   D. Astle, *op.cit.*, 55.

The gist of the first two-thirds of the bill details the necessity to levy a complicated array of new rates, duties and taxes on ships, beer, ale and other liquors. The true purpose of these taxes was that they were needed in order to fund the interest on all future government loans. Shortly thereafter further taxes were introduced including a land tax, paper tax, poll tax, salt tax, stamp tax and window tax, which replaced the hearth or chimney tax. Other taxes initiated were a tax on pedlars, a tax on hackney coaches, a tax on births, marriages and deaths and lastly a tax on bachelors.[47] However, the most punitive tax introduced was an income tax levied at a rate of 20%. It was applied not only to companies, but labourers too.[48]

War and Debt Slavery in Perpetuity

Henceforth a pattern would emerge where unnecessary wars would be embarked upon which simultaneously increased the national debt and the profits of the usurers. Significantly, most of these wars were started against countries, that had implemented interest-free state banking systems, as was the case in the North American colonies and France under Napoléon. This pattern of attacking and enforcing the bankers' system of usury has been deployed widely in the modern era and includes the defeats of Imperial Russia in World War I, Germany, Italy and Japan in World War II and most recently Libya in 2011. These were all countries which had state banking systems, which distributed the wealth of their respective nations on an equitable basis and provided their populations with a standard of living far superior to that of their rivals and contemporaries.

Within two years of its establishment in 1696 the Bank of England had £1,750,000 worth of bank notes circulating with a gold reserve of only 2% or £36,000.[49] On 1 May 1707 the union between Scotland and England was established, motivated in no small way by the necessity to seize control of the Royal Mint in Edinburgh which took place in 1709.

47 A. M. Andreadēs, *op.cit.*, 55.
48 J.E.T. Rogers, *op.cit.*, 106-107.
49 F.J. Irsigler, *op.cit.*, 5.

By 1720 after the conclusion of the War of the Spanish Succession (1701-14) the national debt had risen to £30 million with the war itself having cost £50 million.[50] After the American War of Independence (1775-83), which had been fought after the colonists had been forced to replace their debt – and largely interest-free colonial scrip with English money and had resulted in 50% unemployment, the national debt soared to £176 million. According to Sir John Harold Clapham, who wrote *The Bank of England: A History 1694-1914* in 1944, Solomon de Medina and two da Costas, Fonseca, Henriquez, Mendez, Nuñes, Rodriguez, Salvador and Teixeira de Mattos, who were all Sephardic Jews, had acquired the majority of the bank's shares by 1722.

In 1786 Prime Minister William Pitt the Younger tried to abolish the national debt with a sinking fund which generated interest of £1 million pounds per annum to repay the debt.[51] This scheme was soon abandoned because of the enormous increase in loans incurred to finance the war against Napoléon. In 1797 in order to pay for the burgeoning interest burden, a system of graduated income tax had to be introduced, which by 1815 was yielding £70 million per annum.[52]

The war against France lasted from 1792 until 1815. Among the principal objectives of this pointless bloodletting was to destroy Napoléon's debt- and interest-free system of finance. (See Chapter III). During this period England also waged a war against the United States from 1812 until 1814. This war, as was the case with the war against France, was instigated by England at the behest of banker Mayer Amschel Rothschild (real name Bauer) after the United States Congress refused to renew the charter of the Rothschild-controlled[53] Bank of the United States, which had been the central bank of America from 1791 until 1811.[54] Mayer

---

50   A. M. Andreadès, *op.cit.*, 119.

51   W.D. Bowman, *The Story of the Bank of England*, Herbert Jenkins Ltd, London, 1937, 291.

52   A. M. Andreadès, *op.cit.*, 162.

53   100% of the bank's shares were held by the Rothschilds and their associates.

54   In 1836 President Andrew Jackson closed down the Second Bank of the United States by withdrawing all government deposits. It had received its 20 year charter in 1816.

Amschel Rothschild is famously credited with having said: "Give me control of the economics of a country, and I care not who makes her laws. The few who understand the system, will either be so interested from its profits or so dependent on its favours, that there will be no opposition from that class." British Prime Minister Spencer Perceval (1809-12) tried to stop this completely futile war, but was assassinated on 11 May 1812 in the lobby of the House of Commons by John Bellingham, a political radical, who had been set up by Rothschild.[55]

By 1815 the national debt had ballooned to £885 million. This completely unnecessary war resulted in approximately three million military personnel and at least one million civilians losing their lives. In order to destroy Napoléon's state bank, it cost the deluded British public a staggering £831 million[56] of which over £2.5 billion were still outstanding in 1914. The principal of £504 million had over the intervening period increased fivefold as a result of the compounding effect of interest.

An astute agrarian and parliamentarian William Cobbett (1763-1835) at that time perceived what was afoot and wrote as follows: "I set to read the Act of Parliament by which the Bank of England was created. The investors knew what they were about. Their design was to mortgage by degrees the whole country...lands...houses...property...labour. The scheme has produced what the world never saw before - starvation in the midst of abundance."[57]

The Rothschilds and their associates held 80% of the stock and the US government the balance.

55   www.tomatobubble.com/fh1.html NWO Forbidden History (1765-1816). Concurrent with his appointment as prime minister on 4 October 1809, Perceval also served as Chancellor of the Exchequer, to which office he was appointed on 28 March 1807. He was thus fully acquainted with intricacies of high finance. During his chancellorship his Secretary to the Treasury was John Charles Herries, a personal friend and secret confidant of Nathan Rothschild. See N. Ferguson, *The House of Rothschild, Money's Prophets 1798-1848*, Vol. 1, Penguin Books, London, 1999, 86. (Professor Ferguson is an insider, who attended the 2012 Bilderberg conference held in Chantilly, Virginia, USA).

56   W.D. Bowman, *op.cit.,* 290.

57   W. Cobbett, *The Political Register,* Vol. XVIII, No. 1, London, 14 July, 1810.

In 1800 a member of parliament Sir William Pultney proposed the formation of a national bank after having made "vigorous attacks" against the Bank.[58] In 1824 another member of parliament, David Ricardo, submitted a detailed plan[59] to convert the Bank of England into a national bank. Both attempts failed. The affairs of the Bank of England remained secret and it was not until 1833, 139 years later that a sanitised version of its accounts was presented to parliament by means of the Act of 1833.[60]

At the start of World War I in 1914 the national debt stood at £650 million.[61] On March 31, 1919 it had increased to £7.434 billion[62] of which £3 billion is still outstanding after 95 years at an interest rate of 3.5% per annum. In the 1919 budget 40% of expenditure was allocated to the payment of interest. In World War II the national debt rose by almost 300% from £7.1 billion in 1939 to £20.1 billion in 1945. As at March 2017 it stands at over £1.8 trillion.[63] However, if one includes all liabilities, including state and public pensions, it exceeds £5 trillion.

Nationalisation

On 14 February 1946 the Labour government nationalised the Bank of England. The shareholders received Treasury Notes to the value of £11,015,100 which were redeemable after 20 years.

---

58   *Ibid.*, 207.

59   W.D. Bowman, *op.cit.*, 228 and A. M. Andreadēs, *op.cit.*, 417-427.

60   A. M. Andreadēs, *op.cit.*, xii and 261.

61   A few days after England declared war on 4 August 1914, as an emergency measure £300 million worth of Bradbury pound notes in denominations of 10/- and £1 were issued free of debt and interest. They were soon replaced by war loans. Nobel laureate Professor Frederick Soddy explains the fraudulent manner in which these loans were raised as follows. "The Bank of England issued circulars offering to lend at 3 per cent the money necessary to secure War Loans upon which the taxpayer was to provide 4 per cent. So that for each pound the taxpayer contributed, the bank would receive 15s, and the bogus subscriber 5s. The bank took no risk, for it would hold the new scrip as collateral security for their loan until the debt was redeemed." F. Soddy, *Wealth, Virtual Wealth and Debt*, G. Allen & Unwin, London, 1933, 225.

62   A.N. Field, *op.cit.*, 164-165.

63   www.nationaldebtclocks.com/unitedkingdom.htm

This nationalisation, which supposedly placed the bank under public control, did not introduce any change to the privately run system of fractional reserve banking and was undertaken purely for propaganda purposes, as part of the Labour Party's nationalisation programme of certain financial and industrial concerns.

On 6 April 1974 the Bank of England established the Bank of England Nominees Limited, company registration No. 1307478, a wholly-owned subsidiary, with private shareholders holding its 100 £1 shares, of which 50% were sold. There is a suspicion that this rearrangement of the bank's affairs represents a reverse takeover of it by private shareholders. In view of the fact that certain aspects of the Bank of England's operations are protected by its Royal Charter, Section 27(9) of the Companies Act of 1976 and the Official Secrets Act of 1989, and are therefore not subject to public and parliamentary scrutiny, there may well be substance to this allegation.

Chapter III

Napoléon and the Banque De France

The deadly facts herein revealed lead me to wonder that this monster, interest, has not devoured the whole human race. – Napoléon Bonaparte on being shown an interest table.

France under the Bourbons

When the Bank of England was established in 1694, one of its principal aims was to provide sufficient finance so that England could prosecute its war against France. At that time France was the premier world power both in terms of maritime forces and territorial possessions. Four years previously at the battle of Beachy Head, near Eastbourne, England, the French navy defeated the Anglo-Dutch fleet comprehensively, when it sank twelve ships, while a further twenty ships were exploded by their English crews.[1]

Since 7 June 1654 France had been ruled by its most glorious monarch, King Louis XIV, the Sun King. Louis was well versed in the wiles of the bankers. When he discovered that his Superintendent of Finances, Nicolas Fouquet, was a representative of what we term to-day the money power, and received irrefutable evidence that "he had long been betraying the trust reposed in him by mishandling the State finances and by monstrous corruption", he had him arrested. Fouquet was put on trial and sentenced to complete isolation for the rest of his life in the inaccessible fortress of Pignerol.[2]

---

1   At the battle of Trafalgar, 21 October 1805, the French lost eleven ships.
2   W.G. Simpson, *Which Way Western Man?*, Yeoman Press, Cooperstown, New York, 1978, 230.

Louis XIV, the Sun King, was always wary of bankers. His inability to finance his army and navy with credit led to his defeat in the War of the Spanish Succesion (1702-1714).

The War of the Spanish Succession (1702-1714) was the largest military conflict since the Crusades. It was fought after Louis declared his intention to place his grandson, Philip, Duke of Anjou, on the Spanish throne. This attempt, if successful, would have created a vast Franco-Spanish empire and posed a direct threat to the Bank of England and its proxy, the government of Great Britain. With the ability to create money out of nothing, the English were able to build a large fleet and buy the loyalty of France's enemies by bankrolling them.

Louis held out for nine years, until his heirs suddenly started to die in unnatural circumstances. On 13 April 1711 his heir Louis, Le Grand Dauphin, died allegedly of smallpox, even though he had had the disease when he was a small child. On 12 February 1712 the wife of his grandson, the Duke of Burgundy, died of a fever. A few days later her husband was covered in spots and he died on 18 February 1712 of unknown causes. A few weeks later the King's two great-grandsons fell ill with scarlet fever. The five year old Duke of Brittany died on 18 March 1712. The three year old brother, the Duke of Anjou, survived – miraculously – after the King ordered his isolation and treatment with an antidote.

As a result of these tragedies, the King was persuaded to cease hostilities and commence negotiations. At Utrecht a treaty was signed in March and April 1713 which allowed France to retain largely its pre-war boundaries. Thereafter the heirs to the French throne stopped dying, although this did not prevent the other grandson of Louis, the Duke of Berry, who was the regent of the future Louis XV, dying in an unusual riding "accident".[3] A broken man, the Sun King died of natural causes on 1 September 1715.

The ability of the English to command vast sums of money had not gone unnoticed by the French, who realised that the war had not been won because of a deficiency in financial credit.

---

3   N. Starikov, *Rouble Nationalization The Way to Russia's Freedom*, St Petersburg, Piter, 2013, 57-58.

On 1 May 1716 a Scotsman, John Law, received a patent to open a private bank, the Banque Générale, which was patterned on the Bank of England and which was entitled to issue bank notes and exchange them for gold.[4]

The regent of Louis XV, Phillipe II, Duke of Orléans, realised that this bank could provide government with a means of financing its expenditures and in 1718, France's first central bank came into existence and was renamed the Banque Royale.

The adoption of the Bank of England paradigm of creating money *ex nihilo* soon enabled the French economy to recover and flourish. However, this period of prosperity was of short duration. In January 1720 the French government received a record-breaking loan of 100 million *livres*. The following month news spread suddenly that the bank was experiencing difficulty in exchanging its bank notes for gold coins and an "atrocious panic"[5] ensued. The source of these rumours is not clear, but the most likely suspect would have been the Bank of England which wished to destroy its dangerous rival.[6]

Various attempts were made to shore up the Banque Royale. A decree of 11 March 1720 banned the use of coins from 1 May onwards. When this measure failed to staunch the impending catastrophe, a decree was announced on 22 May 1720 which reduced the value of the bank notes by 50%. A third decree of 10 October 1720 stated that on 1 November bank notes would no longer be used and that they were to be exchanged for state bonds with a further reduction of 50% in their value.

In November 1720 the Banque Royale declared itself bankrupt and its founder and Controller General of Finances, John Law, fled the country the following month. For the Bank of England

---

4   These events are better known as the Mississippi scheme.

5   N. Starikov, *op.cit.,* 59.

6   See Chapter IV page 67 for a description of how the Bank of England destroyed the Assignat currency of revolutionary France.

and its Jewish stockholders, the demise of the Banque Royale was an unmitigated triumph.

Napoléon the Monetary Reformer

Napoléon, who was Emperor of France from 1804 -1815, was very mindful of the fact that money always remains in hiding and only acts through agents, who are often unaware of the aims that they are pursuing. He realised that international money stood behind every foreign enemy, every monarch and every political party, including the Jacobins,[7] stating on one occasion that; "The hand that gives is above the hand that takes. Money has no motherland; financiers are without patriotism and without decency: their sole object is gain."[8] He had very clear ideas as to how he wished the French economy to be run. He defined his system as being for the application of the resources of government, including finances, for the benefit and use of his people for the greater glory of God. His system was for the maintenance of spiritual as against material values, the nation as against political parties, patriotism as against greed, loyalty as against fear.[9]

The bedrock of the economy was to be agriculture – "for that is the soul of the people…the foundations of the Kingdom."[10] Next in importance was industry, which "ministers to the comfort and happiness of the population."[11] A poor third came foreign trade, which only consists of the surplus of agriculture and industry. In his opinion "foreign trade ought to be the servant of agriculture and home industry; these last ought never to be subordinated

---

7   Jacobins were originally members of a revolutionary, extreme left political movement that supported a centralised republic. During the revolution they implemented the Reign of Terror. The Jacobin club was located in Rue Saint-Jacques, Paris.

8   R. McNair Wilson, *Monarchy or Power*, Eyre & Spottiswoode, London, 1934, 92.

9   This is similar to the motto of Vichy France "*travail, famille, patrie*" – work, family, fatherland.

10   R. McNair Wilson, *op.cit.*, 97.

11   *Ibid.*, 97.

Napoléon establishes the Banque de France 18 November, 1800.

to foreign trade."[12] Napoléon's ultimate objective was to ensure not only financial independence, but self-sufficiency in the production of goods for domestic consumption.

Napoléon would not allow loans to be employed for current expenditure, whether civil or military, under any circumstances. On the subject of debt he had this to say:

"One has only to consider what loans can lead to in order to realise their danger. Therefore I would never have anything to do with them and have always striven against them. At one time people asserted that I did not issue loans because I possessed no credit and could find nobody who would lend me anything. That is quite false. That surely implies a very scanty knowledge of human nature and an ignorance of stock exchange methods if people imagine that I could find no one ready to lend. It was not part of my system."[13]

12   *Ibid.*, 97.
13   *Ibid.*, 96.

The State Bank of the French Empire

Napoléon's first act on assuming power as First Consul on 9 November 1799, was to establish the Banque de France on 18 January 1800 as a joint stock company, which commenced operations on 20 February of that year. This Bank replaced the 15, mainly Jewish, private banking houses which had been deeply involved in the events leading up to the Jewish revolution against the French people commonly, but incorrectly, known as the French Revolution 1789-1799[14]. These banks had increased the national debt to £170 million and had charged rapacious rates of interest on loans to the French crown, to the extent that prior to 1789, it was allocating over 50% of its budget expenditure to interest.

The Bank was set up with a share capital of 30 million francs divided into 30,000 shares of 1,000 francs each, of which a portion was subscribed by Napoléon, his family and members of his entourage.[15] The dividend of the shareholders was initially limited to 6% per annum, but was increased in 1806 to two thirds of the bank's profits, with the remaining one third being allocated to the Bank's reserves. The two hundred largest shareholders elected 15 regents or directors, who sat on the General Council administering the Bank and three Censors or inspectors, who supervised management of the Bank. The General Council in turn elected a Central Committee consisting of three members, one of whom was chairman.[16] Napoléon made himself president of the Bank, declaring that "The bank does not belong to the shareholders only; it also belongs to the state, since the state has entrusted to it the privilege of issuing

---

14 C. Quigley, *Tragedy and Hope A History of the World in Our Time*, The Macmillan Company, New York, 1966, 515. According to Sir Walter Scott in *Life of Napoleon*, Vol. 2, "the whole finances of France were brought to a total confusion". See also www. lovethetruth.com/books/pawns/03.htm Chapter Three, The Men Who Caused the French Revolution 1789-1799.

15 www.banque-france.fr/en/banque-de-france/history/the-milestones/1800-creation-of-the-banque-de-france.html

16 A History of Banking in all the Leading Nations; comprising the United States; Russia; Holland; The Scandinavian Nations; Canada; China; Japan; compiled by 13 authors. Edited by the Editor of *The Journal of Commerce and Commercial Bulletin*, New York, 1896, Vol. 3 (France, Italy, Spain, Portugal, Canada).

Treaty of Tilsit - Napoléon and Tsar Alexander I sign the treaty
on a raft on the Neman river.

money. I wish the bank to be in sufficient measure in the hands of
the state, but not too much so."[17]

On 14 April 1803 by means of an Act of parliament, Napoléon
abolished the right of two rival banks, the *Caisse d'Escompte de
Commerce* and the *Comptoir Commercial* to issue bank notes. As
he remarked at that time:

> "Have you not told me that, in order to preserve credit, it is a
> general practice that artificial money, like that of the Bank of
> France, shall issue from only one source? I adopt that idea. A
> single bank can be more easily watched than several concerns
> – both by the Government and the public. With a view to
> emergencies I cannot see any virtue in competition of this
> kind."[18]

On 22 April 1806 a new Act was passed, which replaced the
three member Central Committee with a Governor and two

---

17   *Encyclopedia Britannica*, 1964, Vol. 3, 132.

18   Editor of *The Journal of Commerce and Commercial Bulletin, op.cit.*

Deputy Governors.[19] These appointments were personally vetted by Napoléon. The new Act also increased the Bank's capital to 90 million francs. Napoléon was so suspicious and distrustful of bankers that he personally supervised the operations of the Treasury, lest the secrets of his monetary policies leak out and be exploited by speculators. He was thus his own banker, who controlled both the creation and distribution of money and credit, to the chagrin of the international bankers, particularly the Rothschilds, who were virtually excluded from operating in continental markets. Napoléon made the franc the most stable currency in Europe. After France had abandoned the loan markets of the City of London, a fog of depression settled on its fraternity of bankers and usurers. In typical fashion the English press began to stir up trouble for Napoléon. He was accused of having not observed the conditions of the Treaty of Amiens, which had been signed between England and France on 25 March 1802. Relations broke down when Napoléon refused to sign a trade treaty, which would promote "free trade" and a modern day version of globalisation, and thereby force him to diminish the autarky and isolationism of his continental policy.

England, under the direction of her international bankers, proceeded to bankroll[20] Austria, Prussia, Russia, Spain and Sweden and duly declared war on France. The coalition forces[21] exceeded 600,000. Napoléon could not muster even a third of that number, and would under normal circumstances have been compelled to secure a banker's loan in order to arm and feed them. On 20 December 1803 he trumped the warmongers by selling Louisiana to the United States of America for £3 million. A brief period of peace and prosperity ensued. However, in 1806 a new coalition consisting of England, Russia and Prussia at the initiative of the last named country took to the field. Although the coalition forces were defeated at Jena on 14 October 1806, Napoléon was forced to engage in a series of needless and senseless

---

19   *Ibid.*

20   According to *Encyclopedia Britannica*, 1964, Vol. 19, 573, the Rothschilds "raised" £100 million for the governments of Europe during the Napoléonic wars.

21   This was the first of six different coalition armies.

wars for the next nine years in order to protect France and her new economic dispensation. He promulgated the Continental Blockade, whose objective was to destroy England's export trade, as he realised that England could not finance her imports and fund her allies at the same time.

At the Treaty of Tilsit signed on 7 July 1807 on a raft in the middle of the Neman river in east Prussia, Napoléon and Tsar Alexander I agreed to an alliance which made them the masters of continental Europe. Alexander agreed to join Napoléon's Continental Blockade of England and to provide each other with mutual support in the event of disputes with other nations, and in particular the British Empire. At that time France and Russia were the only two countries in Europe which were not on the usury system and were furthermore not indebted to the Rothschilds. They were therefore the only free and independent nations. However, a few years later Russia started to violate the blockade. This action was premised on the fact that Russia, a producer of mainly raw materials, had very little industrial capacity and had been dependent on England for the importation of industrial products. Alexander was only prepared to continue with the blockade, subject to France supplying him with the industrial goods, which he had previously imported from England. France could not supply these goods, as England commanded the seas and there was no road or rail infrastructure in Europe at that time. Therefore in order to enforce the blockade, Napoléon decided to invade Russia on 24 June 1812 with an army of over 500,000 soldiers. Although he reached Moscow on 14 September 1812, he found that it had been abandoned, and the subsequent winter retreat turned into a major disaster, with only 110,000 of his original army surviving. The following year Napoléon was defeated at the "Battle of the Nations" east of Leipzig on 19 October 1813. On 11 April 1814 he abdicated at Fontainebleau.

After being banished to the island of Elba, situated between Corsica and Tuscany, Napoléon attempted to stage a comeback at the battle of Waterloo in modern day Belgium on 18 June 1815. All the belligerents, England, Prussia and France, were financed by Nathan Rothschild, with France receiving a loan of £10 million.[22] After his defeat Napoléon was exiled to the British island of St Helena in the South Atlantic, where he died under suspicious circumstances, when he was still a fit man at the age of 51, on 5 May 1821. An examination of Napoléon's remains has indicated that he almost certainly died of cyanide poisoning following chronic arsenic intoxication.[23] In such a case it would undoubtedly have been the work of a Rothschild assassin, which conforms to a pattern, repeated consistently during the past two centuries of assassinating all leaders who propose, institute or maintain systems of usury-free banking.[24]

---

22 See N. Ferguson, *The House of Rothschild, Money's Prophets 1798-1848*, Vol. 1, Penguin Books, London, 1999, 95-99, for how the Duke of Wellington's army was financed. In 1936 Eberhard Müller wrote a play *Rothschild Wins at Waterloo*, in which Rothschild intones lines such as "My money is everywhere, and my money is friendly. It is the friendliest power in the world, fat, round as a bullet and smiling"; My fatherland is the London Stock Exchange"; and "The wealth of England is in my hands.", 23.

23 www.napoleon-series.org/ins/weider/c_assassination_w.html The causes of Napoléon's death have been extensively researched by the late Ben Weider, who on 18 February 1998 delivered a lecture entitled *The Assassination of Napoléon* at the Sandhurst Military Academy, London. Weider has identified Comte Charles Tristan de Montholon as the most likely poisoner. He was in constant daily contact with Napoléon and had a dissolute character and a criminal background, which would have provided the perfect profile for a Rothschild assassin. Arsenic which is a colourless, odourless and tasteless substance, would have been most likely added to Napoléon's daily consumption of red wine, which was obtained from the Groot Constantia wine estate near Cape Town. (Cf. The death of Baron Pyotr Wrangel (1878-1928), Commander-in-Chief of the Southern White Russian Army, who was poisoned on the orders of Stalin by the brother of his butler who was staying with the Wrangel family in Brussels, Belgium).

24 Most of the US presidents, who have been assassinated, were involved in monetary reform. They are presidents Abraham Lincoln, James Garfield, William McKinley, Warren G. Harding and John F. Kennedy. President Richard M. Nixon had expressed great interest in reforming the US Federal Reserve Bank while in office, and this may have been a contributing factor to his downfall.

DÉCRET IMPÉRIAL

Concernant les Juifs qui n'ont pas de nom de famille et de prénoms fixes.

À Bayonne, le 20 juillet 1808.

NAPOLÉON, EMPEREUR DES FRANÇAIS, ROI D'ITALIE, et PROTECTEUR DE LA CONFÉDÉRATION DU RHIN;

Sur le rapport de notre ministre de l'intérieur,

Notre Conseil d'État entendu,

Nous AVONS DÉCRÉTÉ et DÉCRÉTONS ce qui suit:

ARTICLE PREMIER.

Ceux des sujets de notre Empire qui suivent le culte hébraïque, et qui, jusqu'à présent, n'ont pas eu de nom de famille et de prénoms fixes, seront tenus d'en adopter dans les trois mois de la publication de notre présent décret, et d'en faire la déclaration par-devant l'officier de l'état civil de la commune où ils sont domiciliés.

As part of Napoléon's plan to assimilate Jews into French society he issued a decree in 1808 ordering all Jews to adopt Surnames, and to use those names on all documents. Napoléon in a letter to his younger brother Jerome, written in 1808 states:

"I have undertaken to reform the Jews, but I have not endeavoured to draw more of them into my realm. ... It is necessary to reduce, if not destroy, the tendency of Jewish people to practise a very great number of activities that are harmful to civilisation and to public order in society in all the countries of the world. It is necessary to stop the harm by preventing it; to prevent it, it is necessary to change the Jews. ... Once part of their youth will take its place in our armies, they will cease to have Jewish interests and sentiments; their interests and sentiments will be French."

Achievements of the French State Banking System

As part of the Code Napoléon (*Code civil des Français*), Napoléon introduced a new commercial code on 21 March 1804. These economic reforms which included substantially reduced taxes, quickly turned the French economy around and resulted in increased trade and the development of new industries, such as cotton-making and sugar beet, which were assisted by tariffs against foreign goods and low interest rate loans. The infrastructure was upgraded on a vast scale not only in France, but throughout western Europe, with the construction of 20,000 miles (32,186 km) of imperial roads and 12,000 miles (19,312 km) of regional roads, almost 1,000 miles (1,609 km) of canals, bridges, the dredging and expansion of harbours such as Cherbourg and Dunkerque, waterworks and public buildings, such as the gallery at the Louvre – all financed with interest free money from the Banque de France.

Napoleon also established an Industrial Board, which provided data and information to French industry; the Imperial University, which administered French education, specialised schools or *lycées* for the study of engineering, science and technology, and professional schools devoted to midwifery, obstetrics and veterinary science.

Napoléon described these accomplishments to his Irish doctor, Barry O'Meara, on the island of St Helena and said that they were his most enduring monument. "The allied powers cannot take from me hereafter the great public works I have executed, the roads which I made over the Alps[25], and the seas I have united. They cannot place their feet to improve where mine have not been before. They cannot take from the code of laws which I formed, and which will go down to posterity."[26]

---

25 Simplon Pass. One of the principal reasons why Napoleon built this pass was to facilitate transportation of his artillery to Italy.

26 I. Tarbell, *A Short Life of Napoléon*, S. S. Mcclure Limited, New York, 1895, Chap. VI Napoléon As Statesman And Lawgiver – Finances – Industries – Public Works. http://

In conclusion we may consider some of Napoléon's achievements, which he communicated to his former chamberlain and constant companion for 18 months on St Helena, Comte de Las Cases:[27]

"I inspired France and Europe with new ideas which will never be forgotten....France's finances are the best in the world. To whom does she owe them? If I had not been overthrown I would have made a complete change in the appearance of commerce as well as of industry. The efforts of the French people were extraordinary. Prosperity and progress were growing immeasurably. Enlightenment was making giant strides. New ideas were everywhere heard and published, for I took pains to introduce science among the people....If I had been given time there would soon have been no more artisans in France; they would all have become artists."[28]

---

history-world.org/Napoléon7.htm

27   Comte Emmanuel Augustin Dieudonné Joseph Las Cases (1766-1842). He recorded Napoléon's reminiscences, reflections and aspirations, which were later published in the *Mémorial de Sainte-Hélène*.

28   R. McNair Wilson, *op.cit.*, 98-99. The author has visited the house where Peter the Great lived for a short while in Zaandam, Holland in 1697. Napoléon visited the house on 13 October 1811 and signed his name with a flourish on one of the interior walls – Napoléon Bonaparte Imperator.

Chapter IV

A Century of Struggle : Rothschild versus the People

Who hold the balance of the World? Who reign
O'er congress, whether royalist or liberal?
Who rouse the shirtless patriots of Spain?
(That make old Europe's journals "squeak and gibber")
Who keep the World, both old and new, in pain
Or pleasure? Who make politics run glibber all?
The shade of Buonaparte's noble daring? —
Jew Rothschild, and his fellow-Christian, Baring.

- Lord Byron, Twelfth Canto

Central Banking in the United States

As this section will show, all previous encounters which the United States has experienced with central banking have been very negative.

During the colonial period the American colonies created their own paper money. The first colony to do so was Massachusetts in 1691. Pennsylvania, New York, Delaware and Maryland soon followed suit. They called their currency colonial script or bills of credit. It freed them from the control of the English banks and enabled them to run their financial affairs in an inflation-free environment with few taxes. Throughout the colonies sustained, stable economic growth and prosperity were achieved, which would not have been possible under a privately run banking system based on usury.

In 1763 American statesman, Benjamin Franklin (1706-1790) visited London, where he was shocked to observe slum

First Bank of the United States built in Philadelphia in 1795. The principal shareholder of the bank was Mayer Amschel Rothschild (1744-1812).

conditions and the wide prevalence of poverty. When the British parliament asked Franklin to explain the source of prosperity of the American colonies, he replied as follows:

"That is simple. In the colonies we issue our own money. It is called colonial script. We issue it in proportion to the demands of trade and industry to make the products pass easily from the producers to the consumers. In this manner, creating for ourselves our own money, we control its purchasing power, and we have no interest to pay anyone."

The following year in 1764 the Bank of England introduced a Currency Bill[1] which severely restricted the colonies right to issue their own money and forbade its legal tender status for the payment of private and public debts. Instead the bank ordered them to issue bonds at interest and sell them to the Bank of England in exchange for English money. In the event only half of the currency was remitted. As a consequence of this law, the

---

1   4 Geo. IIIc. 34

economy of the colonies collapsed and within one year more than half the population became unemployed and destitute. The Stamp Act of 1765 was the last straw, but the abolition of the colonial currency was the primary cause of the revolution.

One of the first tasks entrusted to the Second Continental Congress, which convened for the first time on 10 May 1775, was to issue its own currency, largely to finance its war expenditures. A total of $241,552,788 was issued during the currency's existence. The Bank of England quickly responded. Hundreds of workmen were recruited and soon millions of dollars worth of counterfeit bank notes were rolling off the printing presses and being shipped to New York. The continental dollar retained much of its purchasing power during the first two years of its issuance, but once the English counterfeit bank notes started to increase in circulation, its value soon fell away and by 1780 one dollar was worth only 2.5 cents.

Fifteen years later in 1790 the Bank of England mounted another similar operation, when it employed over 400 workmen in 17 factories in southern and central England to print the *assignat*, which was the currency of revolutionary France. The *assignat* which was backed by clerical lands, was in its initial stages successfully circulated as a means of exchange, and a significant portion of the National Debt was repaid. However, by 1792 the massive infusion of counterfeit notes soon caused the *assignat* to plummet in value and thereafter there was a brief period of hyperinflation. On 14 April 1803 Napoléon Bonaparte introduced the government issued franc which acquired the status of legal tender in 1808.

Already in 1781 before the conclusion of the war of independence on 11 April 1783 Robert Morris (1734-1806), the Superintendent of Finance, introduced a bill which restored the new state to servitude with the establishment of the Bank of North America. This bank commenced operations on 4 January 1782. It attracted large deposits of silver and gold coin and bills of exchange obtained through loans from France and The Netherlands, which enabled it to issue paper currency on the strength of these reserves. Between 1791 and 1796 inflation surged by 72%. In 1795 the State of Pennsylvania withdrew its jurisdiction on account of "alarming foreign influence and fictitious credit".[2]

On 25 February 1791 the Bank of North America was succeeded by a second central bank, which was chartered as the First Bank of the United States. It was imposed as a result of the intrigues of Alexander Hamilton,[3] the Secretary of the Treasury, whose actions indicate that he was working hand in glove with the directors of the Bank of England, as it was modelled on that bank. The new bank had a capital of $10 million, of which 20% was held by the US government and the balance by private investors. The bank was strongly opposed by future presidents John Adams, James Madison and Thomas Jefferson (then Secretary of State), who would later state that:

"The Central Bank is an institution of the most deadly hostility existing against the principles and form of our Constitution...I believe that the banking institutions are more dangerous to our liberties than standing armies. Already they have raised up a moneyed aristocracy that has set the Government at defiance. The issuing power should be taken from the banks and restored to the people to whom it properly belongs. If the American people ever allow the banks to control the issuance of their currency, first by inflation and then by deflation, the banks and corporations that grow up around them will deprive the people of all property until their children will wake up homeless on the continent their fathers occupied."[4]

---

2   T.H. Goddard, *History of Banking Institutions of Europe and the United States*, H.C. Sleight, 1831, 48-50.

3   Hamilton was born of a French Huguenot mother Rachel Faucett Levine on 11 January 1755 or 1757 on the Caribbean island of Nevis in the shadow of Mount Zion. It is probable that Hamilton was not his real name. The author has visited the island and the Hamilton museum.

4   Letter to Major John Cartwright 5 June 1824.

The following year the bank organised the first crash known as the "Panic of 1792". By flooding the market with cheap loans and suddenly calling most of them in, the bank precipitated a 25% plunge in the price of 6% Treasury bonds, which resulted in financial chaos.

By the end of 1795 the bank had lent $6 million to government or 60% of its capital. As the bank was allegedly concerned about the stability of government finances, it demanded partial repayment of this loan. The government did not have the funds available and was therefore forced to sell its shareholding in the bank between the years 1796 and 1802. By means of this cunning ruse, the bank became 100% privately owned, of which 75% of the shares were held by foreigners.

In 1811 the bank's charter came up for renewal. The bank was concealing its profits, operating in a clandestine manner and was believed to be unconstitutional. It was designed primarily to serve the business interests of the north at the expense of the agricultural development of the south, while the Democrats-Republicans (Jeffersonians) wanted to abolish it.

Former president Thomas Jefferson was one of those who "violently opposed"[5] renewal of the bill. What particularly irked the legislators was the fact that the bank was now 100% in the ownership of foreigners. The press variously described the central bank bill as "a great swindle", "a vulture", "a viper" and "a cobra".[6] Furthermore they contended that it was the constitutional right of Congress to regulate weights and measures and issue coined money[7]. The bill was defeated by a wafer thin margin of 65 to 64 votes which was an achievement, as there is a strong likelihood that many of the yes votes were bought. On 3 March 1811 the bank finally closed its doors.[8]

---

5   R. E. Search, *Lincoln Money Martyred*, Omni Publications, Palmdale, California, 1989, (first published in 1935), 38.

6   *Ibid.*, 38-39.

7   US Constitution, Article I, Section 8, Clause 5.

8   http://eh.net/encyclopedia/the-first-bank-of-the-united-states/

When the principal shareholder of the First Bank of the United States, Mayer Amschel Rothschild heard about the deep dissension regarding the renewal of the bank's charter, he flew into a rage and declared that "either the application for renewal of the charter is granted, or the United States will find itself involved in a most disastrous war".[9] He also said that "I will teach those impudent Americans a lesson and bring them back to colonial status". Rothschild tried to influence the British Prime Minister Spencer Perceval into declaring war on the United States in order to resurrect his privately owned central bank.

In 1807 Perceval joined the cabinet as Chancellor of the Exchequer. At that time England was at war with France and one of his principal tasks was to raise money in order to finance the war. Instead of increasing taxes he raised a number of loans, initially from Barings Bank and thereafter mainly from the Rothschilds. Perceval's secretary was John Charles Herries who had been appointed to that position five years previously. Herries[10] was an intimate of Nathan Rothschild and until his death in 1858 faithfully served the Rothschild cause in the various positions he held in the British government as First Lord of the Treasury, Commissary-General to the Army and Chancellor of the Exchequer.

Meanwhile Rothschild *agents provocateurs* were stoking up discontent in North America. In order to provoke the Americans, the British started to interfere with US trade with France, which had imposed a continental blockade against England. As the Royal Navy was short of sailors they engaged in forced recruitment or impressment of American sailors. They also supplied the Indian tribes, and in particular the Shawnee chief, Tecumseh, with arms in order to frustrate and curtail the settlers' westward expansion. The Americans on their part indicated a desire to seize parts of Canada.

---

9   L. Even, *This Age of Plenty, A new conception of economics: Social Credit*, Pilgrims of St. Michael, Rougemont, Quebec, 1996, Chap. 49, History of Banking Control in the United States, 325.

10 N. Ferguson, *The House of Rothschild, Money's Prophets 1798-1848*, Vol. 1, Penguin Books, London, 1999, 86.

Murder of British Prime Minister Spencer Perceval by
Rothschild assassin, John Bellingham.

Concurrently Perceval was facing increased pressure from
Nathan Rothschild to make a declaration of war on the United
States. He refused. The British army was already bogged down
in a stalemate situation in Spain and Portugal (The Peninsular
War 1808-1814) with Napoléon's forces, and he had no desire
to commit more troops and treasure, financed by more interest-
bearing bank loans, simply in order to save Rothschild's sinking
banking interests in America.

The assassin of Spencer Perceval, John Bellingham, was born
about 1769 in St Neots, Huntingdonshire. From 1800-1802 he
worked in Archangelsk as an agent for importers and exporters.
He returned to Russia in 1804, and in November of that year he
was falsely accused of having reneged on a debt of 4,890 roubles
which subsequently led to his imprisonment for four years. On his
release Bellingham took up residence in Duke Street, Liverpool.
He unsuccessfully petitioned the government for compensation.

Bellingham, a bitter and aggrieved man, fell into company with
two dissolute American merchants, Thomas Wilson and Elisha

Peck,[11] who were both keen to have Orders in Council, which forbade neutral nations from trading with France abrogated. These Orders in Council had been introduced by Perceval in response to Napoléon's Continental Blockade which the latter had instituted in 1806 and prohibited trade with Britain and Ireland. Their continuation was due to be debated in parliament on that fateful evening. Thus we observe a confluence of interests, a disturbed and resentful man, two greedy merchants and the puppet master Rothschild pulling the strings in the background.

At 5.15 p.m. on 11 May 1812 as Perceval entered the lobby of the House of Commons, Bellingham stepped forward and shot him in the heart. Perceval collapsed uttering "Murder...... oh my God"[12] and within minutes was dead. Four days later Bellingham was put on trial at the Old Bailey. The trial lasted three days. A plea of insanity was rejected. The brevity of the trial was presumably related to the necessity of preventing any untoward disclosures. As is customary with this type of political assassination the "lone assassin" theory has to be preserved at all costs. On 18 May 1812 Bellingham was hanged. A few weeks later after Perceval's murder the Orders in Council forbidding neutral nations trading with France were revoked.

In the United States House of Representatives, Henry Clay, who was a freemason, led a group of young Democratic-Republicans known as the "War Hawks". The vote to declare war was decided on 1 June 1812 by 79 votes to 49, with all 39 Federalists refusing to support it. In the Senate the vote was decided by 19 to 13 votes. As there was no unanimity, critics frequently referred to it as "Mr Madison's War".

---

11   http://guardian.com/books/2012/may/11/why-spencer-perceval-andro-linklater-review

12   M. Gillen, *Assassination of the Prime Minister: the shocking death of Spencer Perceval*, Sidgwick & Jackson, London, 1972, 185 pp.

In England Perceval's successor, Lord Robert Liverpool, was an enthusiastic supporter of the war. However, neither belligerent was able to achieve its objectives, except Nathan Rothschild, who realised his aim of setting up the Second Bank of the United States on 10 April 1816. When hostilities ceased over two years later on 24 August 1814 over 24,000 lives had been lost. The war was very costly to the United States in financial terms. It incurred a huge war debt of $105 million relative to its population of eight million. As a result thereof the National Debt increased by 182 % from $45 million in 1812 to $127 million in 1815. Peace was signed in Ghent, Belgium on 24 December 1814.

The Second Bank of the United States had an enlarged capital of $35 million. The bank immediately established a large number of branch banks to lend fiat money at compound rates of interest. In 1822 President James Monroe appointed Nicholas Biddle president of the bank.

Biddle had first made contact with the Rothschilds while on government business in Paris in 1804, while acting as secretary to United States minister to France, John Armstrong. As president of the bank he acted as point man to James de Rothschild, who was the bank's principal investor.[13]

The artificially induced recession of 1819-21, which was very profitable for the bankers who were able to buy up assets at depressed prices, convinced the leader of the Democrats, Andrew Jackson, that the only way to terminate these abuses was to close down the central bank. In his re-election campaign in 1832 he declared that "the monster must perish"[14] and his chief slogan was "VOTE ANDREW JACKSON – NO BANK". He stated that "If Congress has the right under the Constitution to issue paper money, it was given to them to be used by themselves not to be

---

13   Patrick Carmack, Bill Still, *The Money Masters: How International Bankers Gained Control of America* (video, 1998), text at http://users.cyberone.com.au/myers/money-masters.html

14   R.V. Remini, *Andrew Jackson*, Twyne Publishers Inc., New York, 1966, 158.

The "People's President", Andrew Jackson, who survived an assassination attempt prior to vetoing a bill that would have renewed the charter for the Rothschild owned Second Bank of the United States.

delegated to individuals or corporations".[15] He also said that "If the American people only understood the rank injustice of our banking and money system – there would be a revolution before morning."

---

15   R.E. Search, *op.cit.*, 43.

Notwithstanding a failed assassination attempt on 30 January 1835 by a presumed Rothschild agent, Richard Lawrence; when the 20 year charter of the Second Bank of the United States came up for renewal in 1836, Jackson collapsed the bank by withdrawing all government deposits. He promptly repaid the National Debt in its entirety, leaving a surplus of $50 million in the Treasury. The central bank was replaced by an Independent Treasury System based on redeemable paper and specie.

During President John Tyler's term of office (1841-45) two attempts were made by Congress under the sponsorship of the former Speaker of the House of Representatives, Henry Clay, to renew the charter of the Bank of the United States. Clay, who had in 1820 become Grandmaster of the Kentucky Lodge,[16] was another agent deemed to be under the influence of the Rothschilds. Tyler vetoed both of these bills and was subsequently inundated with hundreds of letters threatening him with assassination.[17]

For the next 77 years the United States developed without the need of a central bank. Its means of exchange were funded primarily by debt and interest-free Treasury "greenback"[18] dollar bills, first issued by President Abraham Lincoln in 1862 in order to finance his military expenditure during the Civil War, and gold and silver coins.[19] (Up to 1873 gold and silver could be coined at any US mint free of charge). After having rejected offers by private bankers to lend money to the United States government at interest rates varying between 24% and 36% per annum,[20]

---

16   For an exposé of freemasonry see J. Robison, *Proofs of a Conspiracy against all the Religions and Governments of Europe, carried on in the Secret Meetings of Freemasons, Illuminati, and Reading Societies, collected from Good Authorities*, Western Islands, Belmont, Massachusetts, 1967, (first published in 1798), 304 pp.

17   O.P. Chitwood, *John Tyler Champion of the Old South*, Russell & Russell, 1964, (first published in 1939), 249-251.

18   The Confederate government issued its own debt and interest free currency known as "graybacks". They were, however, less successful as large volumes were counterfeited by the Union government.

19   R.E. Search *op.cit.*, 67.

20   *Appleton Cyclopedia*, 1861, 286.

Lincoln had on the advice of his friend Colonel Dick Taylor[21] issued $347 million of currency at no cost to the American people except for the expense of printing and distribution. Lincoln's defiance of Lionel Rothschild and his uncle James resulted in his assassination on the night of 15 April 1865 by John Wilkes Booth[22] (real name Botha) at the behest of the Rothschilds' local agent named Rothberg.

The American Civil War (1861-1865) left the US government with a war debt of $5 billion. As a result of inflation these bonds had declined in value to $2.5 billion. Large quantities of these bonds were bought up by Rothschild's agent August Belmont[23] in the hope of realising them at their face value in gold. In the 1868 presidential election, the Democratic Party candidate, George H. Pendleton, pledged payment only in paper. He was soon replaced by Horatio Seymour on the initiative of Belmont, who had assumed chairmanship of the Democratic National Committee in 1860. Seymour promised payment in specie. However, when the Convention passed a resolution in favour of paper, Belmont was forced to switch sides and thereafter secretly supported the Republican candidate, General Ulysses S. Grant, and used his part ownership of the *New York World* newspaper in order to denigrate and undermine the chances of Seymour. Grant won and on assuming office in 1869 he promptly introduced the Public Credit Act, which paid out the face value on the $5 billion worth of bonds in gold. This resulted in the Rothschilds and their associates making a 100% profit.

The silver exchange was abolished and replaced by a gold standard by means of an Act Revising and Amending the Laws Relative to the Mints, Assay Offices and the Coinage of the United States. On 17 January 1873 this act was passed by

---

21 In a letter written on 16 December 1864, Lincoln thanked Colonel Taylor for his wonderful idea. See Appendix I.

22 R.E. Search, *op.cit.*, 114-31. Booth was said to have been a speaker of the "Hebraic tongue" and frequently attended synagogue services.

23 Born in Alzey, Germany as Schönberg. See also N. Ferguson, *The House of Rothschild, Money's Prophets 1798-1848*, Vol. 1, Penguin Books, London, 1999, 370-375.

the Senate. According to a sworn affidavit of Mr. Frederick A. Luckenbach dated 9 May 1892, he had learnt from Mr. Ernest Seyd in London that the demonetisation of American silver had been expressly ordered by the Governors of the Bank of England, who had furthermore paid £100,000 ($500,000) in order to have a sufficient number of committee members of the US Congress dealing with financial matters bribed.[24] This nefarious deed became known as the "Crime of 1873".

The forced abandonment of the people's money, silver, was also instituted in the German Empire when the government inexplicably ceased to mint silver *thaler* coins in 1871. There seems to be little doubt that this was part of a synchronised scheme co-ordinated by the Rothschilds in order to further entrench the gold standard.[25]

The gold standard wrought havoc on the American economy and enabled private bankers to withhold loans and restrict the money supply at will. There followed a series of unnaturally created panics or bank runs in 1873, 1884, 1890-1, 1893-4, 1897, 1903 and 1907.[26] These artificially created bank runs so incensed President James Abram Garfield that shortly after he took office on 4 March 1881, he issued a statement in the middle of June of

24 *Ibid.,* 66-68. This event was later described in a novel, by W.H. Harvey, Coin Publishing Company, 1894. "The hard core of the conspiracy is that the London bankers, who were also Jewish, decided to destroy the United States by the manipulation of the currency. In *A Tale of Two Nations* the story is cast in the form of a melodramatic novel in which the spider at the centre is B Rothe, a name, the significance of which was not lost on a generation which had heard a great deal about the doings of the Rothschilds. Rothe, decides that for personal gain and to prevent America from becoming strong financially he must bring about the demonetisation of silver." R. Gollam, *The Commonwealth Bank of Australia: Origins and Early History,* Australian National University Press, Canberra, 1968, 45-46.

25 See *Official Proceedings of the Democratic National Convention,* Held in Chicago, Illinois, July 7, 8, 9, 10, and 11, 1896, (Logansport, Indiana, 1896), 226-234 where former Congressman William Jennings Bryan delivered his famous *Cross of Gold* speech. "...we shall answer their demands for a gold standard by saying to them, you shall not press down upon the brow of labor this crown of thorns. You shall not crucify mankind upon a cross of gold"

26 C.A. Lindbergh, *The Economic Pinch (Lindbergh on the Federal Reserve),* The Noontide Press, Costa Mesa, California, 1989, (first published in 1923), 93-94.

President James Abram Garfield (right) was gunned down by "lone assassin" Charles J. Guiteau at the main railway station in Washington on 2 July 1881.

that year that he intended to master the problem, when he said the following:

"Whosoever controls the volume of money in any country is absolute master of all industry and commerce... And when you realize that the entire system is very easily controlled, one way or another, by a few powerful men at the top, you will not have to be told how periods of inflation and depression originate".[27]

Two weeks later Garfield was gunned down by "lone assassin" Charles J. Guiteau who had a grievance for not having received a diplomatic posting. Garfield did not die immediately, but as a result of improper medical care, quite possibly done so deliberately, lingered on until his death on 19 September 1881. At his trial the hidden hand of Rothschild was revealed when Guiteau claimed "that important men in Europe put him up to the task, and had promised to protect him if he were caught".[28]

---

27   E. H. Brown, *The Web of Debt The Shocking Truth About Our Money System And How We Can Break Free*, Third Millenium Press, Baton Rouge, Louisiana, 2008, 96.

28   http://en.wikipedia.org/wiki/James_A._Garfield

The 1907 panic had the worst effects. In early 1907 Jacob Schiff, CEO of Kuhn, Loeb & Co. warned that "Unless we have a Central Bank with adequate control of credit resources, this country is going to undergo the most severe and far reaching money panic in history."[29] In October of that year JP Morgan, another Rothschild front man, set the panic in motion by circulating rumours that its rival, the Knickerbocker Bank and Trust Co. was insolvent. In the ensuing crash shares listed on the New York Stock Exchange lost 50% of their value. Further consequences of this deliberately induced panic were a 11% drop in industrial production the following year, a 26% rise in imports and an increase in unemployment from under 3% to 8%. It was these continual phases of artificially created boom and bust, inflation and deflation, which provided the motivation and pretext to set up a central bank, which would allegedly solve all these never ending problems for all time.

Establishment of the United States Federal Reserve Bank

In order to mislead the public two "alternative" plans were proposed. One was advanced by the National Monetary Commission under leadership of Senator Nelson Aldrich (grandfather of Nelson Aldrich Rockefeller) and known as the Aldrich Plan. The other plan adopted by the Special Currency Committee of the New York Chamber of Commerce was under the chairmanship of Paul Warburg, a German Jewish banker, who was acting on behalf of the Rothschild interests headed by Baron Alfred Rothschild. It was known as the Wall Street Plan. Except for the distribution of reserves, both plans were identical and had as their aim the establishment of a central reserve bank.

On 22 November 1910 the banking conspirators including among others A. Piatt Andrew, Assistant Secretary of the Treasury, Frank Vanderlip, president of the National City Bank of New York, Henry P. Davidson, senior partner JP Morgan and

29   Speech given to New York Chamber of Commerce.

Senator Robert Marion "Fighting Bob" La Follette who did all in his power to prevent passage of the Banking and Currency Bill and its planned enslavement of the American people.

Company, Charles D Norton, president First National Bank of New York, Benjamin Strong, vice president Bankers Trust of New York and Paul Moritz Warburg, partner Kuhn, Loeb & Company, sneaked out of New York in Aldrich's Pullman car (with all its blinds drawn) from Hoboken, New Jersey railway station to Jekyll Island, Georgia.[30] At the very exclusive Jekyll Island Hunt Club owned by JP Morgan, the fate of the American people and indeed the world would be determined over the next ten days by the this group of criminally inclined financiers, who were also known as the First Name Club. Only first names were used so as not to reveal their identities to the staff.[31]

The bill to establish the United States Federal Reserve Bank was vehemently opposed by Congressman Charles August Lindbergh who said that:

> "This act establishes the most gigantic trust on earth, such as the Sherman Anti-Trust Act would dissolve if Congress did not by this act expressly create what by that act it prohibited. When the president signs this act the invisible government by the money power, proven to exist by the [Pujo] Money Trust investigation, will be legalized. The greatest crime of Congress is its currency system. The schemiest legislative crime of all ages is perpetuated by this new banking and currency bill."[32]

The bill was bitterly opposed in the Senate, with Senator Robert M. La Follette being one of its most "vociferous opponents".[33] It was passed into law on 23 December 1913, after the members of the Senate had been threatened by the thoroughly disreputable President Woodrow Wilson, "who was as devoid of ethics and principle as he was of morality",[34] that he would keep them in

---

30 H.S. Kenan, *The Federal Reserve Bank*, The Noontide Press, Los Angeles, 1968, 92-99.

31 *Ibid.*, 104.

32 *The Senate*, Vol. 51, November 1912.

33 E.M. Josephson, *The "Federal" Reserve Conspiracy & Rockefellers*, Chedney Press, New York, 1968, 52.

34 *Ibid.*, 43. President Wilson was a victim of Jewish blackmail. See M.C. Piper, The Making of Woodrow Wilson – An American Nero?, *The Barnes Review*, Washington

session until it had passed the bill and deny them their Christmas recess. Only a minority of 43 Senators supported the bill, with 25 voting against it, 27 refusing to vote and 5 members absent. The promoters of the bill promised that the United States dollar would become a stable currency and that business cycles and recessions would become a thing of the past.

In the event since the inception of the US Federal Reserve Bank in 1914, the US dollar has lost 97% of its purchasing power and there have been 19 recessions, the great depression of the 1930s and the current great recession which started in 2008, and notwithstanding main stream media propaganda to the contrary, appears to have all the symptoms of a depression. Since 1910 the National Debt has increased from $2.65 billion to $20 trillion in March 2017, while unfunded liabilities such as social security, Medicare and benefits for military veterans exceed $240 trillion[35].

The United States Federal Reserve Bank instead of functioning as the people's banker of the bankers, has operated solely as a private bank for the benefit of private bankers. It comes as no surprise that in its 104 years of existence its accounts have never been submitted to public audit.[36] The following are the bank's principal shareholders:[37] Rothschild Banks of London and Berlin, Lazard Brothers Banks of Paris, Israel Moses Sieff Banks of Italy, Warburg Bank of Hamburg and Amsterdam, Shearson American Express, Goldman Sachs of New York, JP Morgan Chase Bank.[38]

D.C., Vol. VI, No. 2, March/April, 2000, 6-12.

35   http://www.thecommonsenseshow.com/2014/08/05/the-statistics-do-not-lie-welfare-is-the-best-paying-entry-level-job-in-35-states/

36   On 25 July 2012 a proposal by Congressman Dr. Ron Paul (Republican, Texas) that the US Federal Reserve Bank be subjected to a transparent public audit was passed by 327 to 98 votes. As he remarked at the time, 'I think that they [the Federal Reserve] can deal in trillions of dollars and know that nobody is allowed to ask them a question is a moral hazard. And this removes that moral hazard.' *USA Today*, On Politics.

37   The House of Rothschild is currently the majority shareholder with a stake of 58%. See E. Mullins, *The Secrets of the Federal Reserve*, Bankers Research Institute, Staunton, Virginia, 1993, 47-62.

38   On 20 June 1992 JP Morgan acquired Manufacturers Hanover Trust Company and the latter's shareholding in the US Federal Reserve Bank.

The State Bank of the
Russian Empire

Meanwhile across the Atlantic a different system of finance, viz. state banking, had been adopted. From September 1814 to June 1815 the Congress of Vienna was held in order to settle the issues arising from the French Revolutionary Wars, the Napoléonic Wars and the dissolution of the Holy Roman Empire. Behind the scenes Nathan Mayer Rothschild proposed the formation of a new world order concentrated around central banking. All the major powers, with the exception of Russia, were indebted to the Rothschild banks. Tsar Alexander I (1801-25) refused to comply with Rothschild's devious scheme and derailed it. Instead he established The Holy Alliance between Austria, Prussia and Russia, which was signed on 26 September 1815 by Emperor Francis I of Austria, King Friedrich Wilhelm III of Prussia and Tsar Alexander. He also rejected Rothschild's offer to set up a central bank in Russia. Whether it was because he distrusted this shady banker or was aware of the perils of central banking is not known, but he wisely declined. However, his prudent behaviour incurred the vindictive and unrelenting wrath of the Rothschilds, who according to Major-General Count Cherep-Spiridovich,[39] were responsible for the assassination of the last five Tsars and would seek and obtain their Talmudic vengeance in spectacular fashion 102 years later.

On 12 June 1860 The State Bank of the Russian Empire[40] was founded with the aim of boosting trade turnovers and the strengthening of the monetary system. Up to 1894 it was an auxiliary institution under the direct control of the Ministry of Finance. In that year it was transformed into being the banker of

---

39   Maj.-Gen. Count A. Cherep-Spiridovich, *The Secret World Government or "The Hidden Hand"*, The Anti-Bolshevist Publishing Association, New York, 1926, 41. Not one of these tsars reached an old age. Their average age at death was 53. See also S. Goodson *Murdering the Czars: The Rothschild Connection*, *The Barnes Review*, Washington D.C., Vol. XX, No. 5, September/October 2014, 38-40.

40   A. Del Mar, *Money and Civilization: Or a History of the Monetary Laws and Systems of Various States Since the Dark Ages, and Their Influence upon Civilization*, Omni Publications, Hawthorne, California, 1975 (first published in 1886), 313.

the bankers and operated as an instrument of government's policy. It minted and printed the nation's coins and notes, regulated the money supply and through commercial banks provided industry and commerce with low interest rate loans. Its vast gold reserves, the largest in the world, exceeded the bank note issue by more than 100%, except for the year 1906. By 1914 it had become one of the most influential lending institutions in Europe.[41]

Not unexpectedly Russia had the smallest national debt in the world. The following table reflects the number of rubles of debt per inhabitant.

France	Great Britain	Germany	Russia
288.0	169.8	135.6	58.7

By 1914 83% of the interest and amortisation of the national debt, of which less than 2% was held abroad, was funded by the profits of the Russian State Railways. In 1916 the total length of the main lines was 100,817 *verst* or kilometres. Russian commercial and canal tonnage of 11,130,000 in 1910 exceeded British merchant tonnage of 10,750,000.

In 1861 Tsar Alexander II (1855-81)[42] abolished serfdom, which at that time affected 30% of the population. By 1914 very little land remained in the possession of the Russian estate owners, who were mainly the nobility. 80% of the arable land was in the hands of the peasants, which had been ceded to them for a very small sum. This land was held in trust by the village commune or *mir*. However, after the passing of the Stolypin[43] Act in 1906, peasants could obtain individual title with hereditary rights. By 1913 two million families had availed themselves of this

---

41   The State Bank of the Russian Empire, The Central Bank of the Russian Federation, 12 Neglinnaya Street, Moscow 107016.

42   On 13 March 1881 Tsar Alexander II was assassinated in St Petersburg by members of a Jewish terrorist organisation *Narodnaya Volya* (The People's Will).

43   Pyotr Arkadyevich Stolypin (1862-1911) was prime minister of Russia 1906-11. On 18 September 1911 he was assassinated by a Jewish terrorist Dmitri Bogrov (real name Mordechai Gershkovich).

opportunity to acquire what became known as "Stolypin farms." Nearly 19,000,000 acres (7,689,027 hectares) were allotted to these individual peasant proprietors by the land committees[44]. The Peasants' State Bank, which was described at that time as the "greatest and most socially beneficent institution of land credit in the world"[45] granted loans at a low rate of interest, which was in effect a handling charge. Between 1901 and 1912 these loans increased from 222 million rubles to 1.168 billion rubles.

Agricultural production soared so that by 1913, Russia had become the world's bread basket as the following table reveals.

	World Production	Russian Production	%
Barley	1,771.4	750.04	42.3
Oats	3,324.6	1,087.00	30.3
Rye	2,378.0	1,593.00	67.0
Wheat	4,971.4	1,554.80	31.2

Russian agricultural production of cereals exceeded the combined production of Argentina, Canada and the United States by 25%. In 1913 Russia had 37.5 million horses – more than half of all those in the world. She also produced 80% of the world's flax and provided more than 50% of the world's egg imports. Mining and industrial output also expanded by huge margins. Between 1885 and 1913 coal production increased from 259.6 million poods[46] to 2,159.8 million poods, cast iron production rose from 25 million poods in 1890 to 1,378 million poods in 1913 and petroleum production rose from 491.2 million poods in 1906 to 602.1 million poods in 1916. From 1870 to 1914 industrial output grew by 1% per annum in Great Britain, 2.75% per annum in the United States and 3.5% per annum in Russia. During the period from 1890 to 1913 industrial production quadrupled and

---

44 G. Buchanan, *My Mission to Russia and Other Diplomatic Memories,* Cassell and Company Limited, London, 1923, 161.

45 G. Knupffer, *The Struggle for World Power, Revolution and Counter-Revolution*, The Plain-Speaker Publishing Company, London, 1971, 230.

46 1 pood = 16.38kg

Russian industries were able to satisfy 80% of internal demand for manufactured goods – a perfect example of autarky. Throughout the last 20 years of peacetime imperial rule (1895-1914) the increase in Gross Domestic Product averaged 10% per annum.

With the Russian State bank creating the people's money out of nothing at almost zero interest; as opposed to the rest of the world where central banks allowed parasitic private banks to create their nation's money supply at usurious rates of interest, it comes as no surprise to find that in 1912 Russia had the lowest levels of taxation in the world. These very low rates of taxation also attest to the efficiency of the Russian government. Furthermore throughout this period of state banking there was no inflation and no unemployment.

Direct Taxes in Rubles per Inhabitant

	State Taxes %	Local Taxes %	Total %
Great Britain	10.01	16.74	26.75
Germany	5.45	7.52	12.97
France	6.44	5.91	12.35
Austria	5.12	5.07	10.19
Russia	1.28	1.38	2.66

Indirect Taxes in Rubles per Inhabitant

	State Taxes %	Local Taxes %	Total %
Great Britain	13.86	-	13.86
Germany	9.31	.33	9.64
France	13.11	2.89	16.00
Austria	9.9	1.38	11.28
Russia	5.95	.03	5.98

Between 1897 and 1913 state receipts rose from 1.400 million gold rubles[47] to 3.471 million gold rubles. By 1914 the surplus on the budget account was 512 million gold rubles and there was no increase in taxation. Throughout this same period the foreign trade balance between exports and imports was in surplus. An indication of the financial health of the Russian economy can be gauged from the following comparative table of gold reserves. The gold reserves and bank notes are expressed in millions of roubles. The gold reserves and bank notes are expressed in millions of roubles.

Gold Reserves

	Gold	Banknotes
The State Bank of the Russian Empire	1,550	1,494
Banque de France (Central bank)	1,193	2,196
Reichsbank (Central bank)	411	930
Bank of England (Central bank)	331	263

An independent study by British lawyers concluded that the Russian Code of Laws and judiciary were "the most advanced and impartial in the world."[48] Elementary education was obligatory and free right up to university level, where only nominal fees were charged. Between 1906 and 1914 10,000 schools were opened annually. Russian universities were renowned for their high academic standards.

In labour relations the Russians were pioneers. Child labour was abolished over 100 years before it was abolished in Great Britain in 1867. Russia was the first industrialised country to pass laws limiting the hours of work in factories and mines. Strikes, which were forbidden in the Soviet Union, were permitted and minimal in Tsarist times. Trade union rights were recognized in 1906, while an Inspectorate of Labour strictly controlled working conditions in factories. In 1912 social insurance was introduced. Labour laws were so advanced and humane that President William

---

47   1 ruble = two shillings gold; 9.4 rubles = £1.

48   G. Knupffer, *op.cit.*, 139-40.

His Imperial Majesty Tsar Nicholas II. His State Bank of the Russian Empire bestowed on his people abundance and benefits unparalleled in the history of mankind.

The State Bank of the Russian Empire in 12 Neglinnaya Street, Moscow. This same building now houses the The Central Bank of the Russian Federation.

Taft of the United States was moved to say that "the Emperor of Russia has passed workers' legislation which was nearer to perfection than that of any democratic country."[49] The people of all races in the Russian Empire had an equality of status and opportunity, which was unparalleled in the modern world. His Imperial Majesty Tsar Nicholas II (1868-1917) and his state bank had created a workers' paradise that was unrivalled in the history of mankind.

On 17 November 1917, the Rothschilds, fearful that replication of this extraordinary example of freedom and prosperity would destroy their malevolent banking empire, instigated and financed a Judeo-Bolshevik revolution in Russia,[50] which wrecked and ruined a wonderful country and resulted in the deaths by murder and starvation, according to Alexander Solzhenitsyn, of 66 million innocent people.[51]

49   *Ibid.*, 142.

50   W.S.L. Churchill, Zionism versus Bolshevism. A Struggle for the Soul of the Jewish People, *Sunday Illustrated Herald*, 8 February 1920. Churchill blamed the revolution on a "world conspiracy for the overthrow of civilisation and for the reconstitution of society on the basis of arrested development, of envious malevolence and impossible equality, [which] has been steadily growing.... It has been the mainspring of every subversive movement during the Nineteenth Century; and now at last this band of extraordinary personalities from the underworld of the great cities of Europe and America have gripped the Russian people by the hair of their heads and become practically the undisputed masters of that enormous empire."

51   According to Swiss historian, Jürgen Graf, Solzhenitsyn employed a statistician, Professor Alexeevich Kurganov, who calculated the number of deaths at 66 million. In *The American Hebrew Magazine* of 10 September 1920 it was stated that "The Bolshevik

The Creation and Control of the Soviet Union

In *Wall Street and the Bolshevik Revolution*[52] author, Professor Antony Sutton, with the assistance of State Department documents and personal papers of American international bankers, details the "enthusiastic alliance of Wall Street and Marxist Socialism".[53] Without the financial support of J P Morgan's Guaranty Trust Company, John D Rockefeller's Chase National Bank, Jacob's Schiff's Kuhn Loeb and Company and Olf Aschberg of the Swedish Nya Banken[54], the Judeo-Bolshevik revolution would not have succeeded. Of more particular interest in the financing of the revolution is the role which Maxim Litvinov (1876-1951), who was born Meyer-Genokh Mojsjewicz Wallach-Finkelstein, played as a "revolutionary" in destroying Imperial Russia and handing it over to the international bankers.

Litvinov commenced his revolutionary career in 1898. In 1901 he was arrested and spent 18 months in prison from which he escaped. In 1903 he was entrusted with money, which was used to finance and distribute the newspaper of the Russian Socialist Democratic Party, *Iskra*,[55] which was printed in London. In 1905 Litvinov received further funds from "friends from abroad",[56] which enabled the purchase of arms – again in London. Thereafter Litvinov, now known as *Papasha* or Daddy[57], became the source of all foreign funds and was appointed treasurer of the party – a decision which Lenin could not overrule, because Litvinov was a representative of the Rothschilds with powers

---

Revolution in Russia was the work of Jewish planning and Jewish dissatisfaction. Our Plan is to have a New World Order. What worked so wonderfully in Russia is going to become Reality for the whole world."

52   A. C. Sutton, *Wall Street and the Bolshevik Revolution*, Arlington House Publishers, New Rochelle, New York, 1981.

53   *Ibid.*, 16.

54   In 1918 the bank was renamed Svensk Ekonomiebolaget.

55   Russian for a spark. It was also published in various West European cities from 1900-1905.

56   N. Starikov, *Rouble Nationalization The Way to Russia's Freedom*, St Petersburg, Piter, 2013, 189.

57   *Ibid.*, 190.

exceeding those of Lenin. Lenin was merely informed of the decision. A few months later at a meeting in Geneva, Litvinov was elected Secretary of Foreign Transport Groups. Lenin was again informed of this decision. Litvinov was never a genuine revolutionary, but instead used Bolshevism as a disguise in order to advance the aims of his master's agenda.

From 1908-1918 Litvinov resided in London with the assistance of his "English friends".[58] During this period he held a variety of occupations working for a publishing house, Williams and Norgate, a tourist agency and selling farm machinery. Presumably these occupations provided a suitable cover for his clandestine activities. In 1914 at the outbreak of World War I, the Russian government demanded that all its citizens be returned to Russia in order to serve in the army. However, the British authorities allowed Litvinov to remain. In 1916 Litvinov married a daughter of one of the most distinguished Jewish families in England, Ivy Low. On 3 January 1918 Litvinov was appointed as the authorised representative of Soviet Russia. One of his first tasks was to demand that the money held at the Bank of England on behalf of the Tsarist embassy be handed over to him. The bank duly complied.

In September 1918 a conspiracy against the Bolsheviks involving British ambassador Robert Bruce Lockhart, was exposed. Both Lockhart and Litvinov were arrested by their respective governments and as a result of a subsequent exchange, Litvinov returned to Moscow. His new assignment was "to secure fast outflow of gold and jewellery from Russia"[59] via Scandinavia, under the cover of a scheme to purchase steam engines later known as "gold engines". A quarter of Russia's gold reserves were transferred to Sweden for onward transhipment. For the Rothschilds it was now retribution time.

On 21 April 1921 Litvinov was appointed Commissioner of the Council of People's Commissars for currency transactions and

58   *Ibid.*, 188.
59   *Ibid.*, 194.

Maxim Litvinov (born Wallach-Finkelstein) For over 40 years he was Rothschild's bag-man. He paved the way and assisted in the looting of Russia by the international bankers.

sales of gold abroad. "Several hundred millions [roubles] of our gold went through my hands and was sold abroad. I sold the majority of this gold directly or through various intermediaries to large French companies which re-melted this gold either in France or Switzerland, and then this gold went to its final destination in storage at the American Reserve Bank"[60] - Rothschild's privately-owned bank! Litvinov had become the "authorised representative of the bankers – owners of the FRB, the Bank of England and Soviet Russia"[61]. As can be seen the Bolshevik Revolution was little more than a giant asset stripping exercise by the Rothschilds.

In December 1921 the Kuzbass Autonomous Industrial Colony was established. It handed over control of a vast industrial complex to a group of American and European investors who had assisted in financing it. Thereafter "millions of gold rubles flowed abroad without any customs duties, allegedly, as interest

60   *Ibid.,* 199.
61   *Ibid.,* 203.

for the capital invested by European bankers",[62] despite the fact that the investments were not all that large.

In 1924 Josef Stalin became the leader of the Soviet Union, but Litvinov, who feared no one, remained pre-eminent. His rudeness to Stalin was legendary.[63] In the purge of 1937-1938 nearly all of Litvinov's deputies were arrested and then shot. Litvinov pleaded for the life of one of his closest friends, Boris Stomonyakov, and informed Stalin that he could vouch for him. Stalin looked Litvinov in his eyes and replied: "Comrade Litvinov you can only vouch for yourself".[64]

From 1930-1939 Litvinov was People's Commissar for Foreign Affairs of the Soviet Union. In 1939 relations between National Socialist Germany and the Soviet Union started to thaw a little. This was anathema to Litvinov's masters, who had nightmarish memories of the Holy Alliance struck between Austria, Prussia and Russia in 1815 and Bismarck's *Dreikaiserbund* (Three Emperors league) concluded between the same three empires in 1872. Litvinov objected, but by this time Stalin had had enough of Litvinov's impudent behaviour. On 3 May 1939 a quiet *coup d'etat* took place and Stalin "dismissed the puppet of the banking underworld from the position of foreign minister"[65]

With its own State Bank of the USSR or *Gosbank*, which was founded on 16 November 1921, the Soviet Union had finally gained its sovereignty and independence from the international bankers. All Litvinov's deputies and heads of departments were arrested, but he himself was spared, as he was untouchable. Litvinov was allowed to retire to his *dacha*, but was kept under constant surveillance.

---

62   *Ibid.*, 204.
63   *Ibid.*, 205, 206 and 209. In June 1941 at a meeting of foreign diplomats, Litvinov arrived dressed in a sumptuous suit of fleece. Stalin asked him why he was not wearing a dark suit like everyone else. Litvinov replied cheekily: "It has been eaten by the moths".
64   *Ibid.*, 206.
65   *Ibid.*, 207.

In late 1941 Litvinov's services were once again required. With the Germans banging on the gates of Moscow, Stalin's desperate situation necessitated urgent help from the West. Litvinov was sent to Washington as Soviet ambassador. The Americans were reluctant to lend money to the Soviet Union, but Litvinov soon sorted everything out and within a few weeks a loan of one billion dollars was granted. A Lend Lease agreement was signed and over the next four years $11 billion worth of supplies and services were provided. Litvinov "could call the White House at any time and the President [Roosevelt] would see him immediately".[66] Both these stooges of the international bankers pumped gold – the one out of Russia, the other from the people of the United States – into the vaults of Rothschild's Federal Reserve Bank.[67]

Litvinov[68] was recalled in 1943 when the war turned in Russia's favour. His successor as foreign minister, Vyacheslav Molotov, provides an apt epitaph. "Litvinov was utterly hostile to us … He deserved the highest measure of punishment at the hands of the proletariat. Every punishment".[69]

From 1-22 July 1944 the international bankers organised a conference at Bretton Woods, New Hampshire. Its purpose was to establish a World Bank and an International Monetary Fund which would govern relations amongst independent nations and maintain fixed exchange rates. Soviet representatives attended the conference, but refused to sign, stating that the proposed institutions were "branches of Wall Street".[70] This impertinence of Stalin in all probability angered the Rothschilds, but there was little that they could do, while Germany remained undefeated.

---

66   Litvinov served as ambassador from 10 November 1941 to 22 August 1943.

67   N. Starikov, *op.cit.*, 211. On 5 April 1933 by means of Executive Order 6102 the United States government confiscated all privately-owned gold, with the exception of numismatic coins, and exchanged it for paper money.

68   It comes as no surprise that Litvinov refused to write any memoirs.

69   F. Chuev and A. Resis, *Molotov Remembers,* Chicago, 1993, 68.

70   E.S. Mason and R.E. Asher, *The World Since Bretton Woods: The Origins, Policies, Operations and Impact of the International Bank for Reconstruction,* Washington D.C., Brookings Institution, 1973, 29.

Between 17 July and 2 August 1945 the Potsdam conference was held in Germany. It determined the new borders of Europe. From this time the Soviet Union was gradually frozen out and the start of the Cold War commenced. Stalin had no designs on Western Europe. His army was completely exhausted and he had more than enough tasks on his hands in absorbing Eastern Europe under his hegemony and repairing all the damage to his country, which he had inflicted on himself by provoking Germany into starting a preventative war.[71] From a military perspective the dropping of alleged[72] nuclear bombs on Hiroshima and Nagasaki was unnecessary, as in January 1945 Japan was already trying to secure surrender terms. The firebombing of these two cities served two more sinister purposes: (i) as a punishment to the Japanese for having set up their own state bank and (ii) as a warning to the Soviet Union which also had a state bank.

The Cold War was prosecuted, initially, by the Western countries in order to bring the Soviet Union to heel. Stalin, who was rather more of a nationalist[73] than a communist, resisted and was allegedly poisoned, and then allowed to die from a massive stroke for which he did not receive any medical treatment, on 1 March 1953[74]. Thereafter the Cold War degenerated into a farce, as the West, and in particular the United States, invested heavily in the Soviet Union. Huge investments were made at the Gorki plant which built Ford trucks, and the largest automotive plant in the world at Volgograd, which manufactured Fiat cars. There were also substantial investments in aviation, computers and electricity. The Soviet Union

---

71 Stalin planned to attack Germany on 6 July 1941 and named it Operation *Groscha* (Storm). See V. Suvorov, *The Chief Culprit Stalin's Grand Design to Start World War II*, Naval Institute Press, Annapolis, Maryland, 2008, 328 pp. Suvorov is of the opinion "that the Soviet Union lost World War II", 280.

72 See http://heiwaco.tripod.com/bomb.htm and http://aetherforce.com/nuclear-bomb-hoax/ On 29 August 1949 Stalin faked his own atomic bomb with uranium ore supplied by Wismut AG, Aue, Saxony, DDR at Semipalatinsk, Kazakh SSR.

73 See K. Bolton, *Stalin, The Enduring Legacy*, Black House Publishing, London, 2012, 164 pp.

74 S.S. Montefiore, *Stalin The Court of the Red Tsar*, Weidenfeld & Nicolson, London, 2005, 651-665. Stalin's stroke may have been induced by the addition of wafarin, a blood-thinning drug, to his wine over the previous days.

became an investment destination of choice. The Russians soldiered on, but with 50% of their budget being allocated to armaments, this was a war which they could not win in the long term. This explains why living standards in the Soviet Union could never match those achieved in the West, notwithstanding the provision of free services such as education and housing.

In 1991 the Soviet Union imploded and a swarm of advisers arrived from the USA, who introduced the wonders of unregulated free market capitalism which included income tax and usury. The primary purpose of these advisers was "to present the law on the Central Bank of Russia at the right moment which hardly did less damage than a whole army of invaders in making Russia lose its sovereignty".[75] For almost 200 years the Tsars and Soviets resisted, but finally Russia fell entirely into the hands of the Rothschilds.

Rothschilds' Responsibility for the Anglo-Boer War

Throughout the nineteenth century the world's monetary system was based on the gold standard, which had been developed and maintained by the Rothschilds. The discovery of the largest goldfields in the world on the Witwatersrand in 1886 created a new source of supply, which had to be controlled, if this dishonest financial system was to survive. Unfortunately for the Rothschilds these new mines were located in the independent *Zuid-Afrikaansche Republiek*.

Streams of immigrants and speculators soon arrived in the country. Some of them were British, but a larger number consisted of "mostly Russian, Polish and German Jews, with roving propensities and no strongly rooted attachment to an old country".[76] The gold

---

75   N. Starikov, *op.cit.*, 182-183.

76   J.A. Hobson, *The War in South Africa Its Causes and Effects*, James Nisbet & Co.,
     Limited, London, 1900, 70. Hobson mentions on page 12 that in the Johannesburg
     Directory of 1899, 24 Joneses, 53 Browns and 68 Cohens were listed.

mine owners were almost entirely Jewish. The leading company was the Eckstein group named after its managing director, Hermann Eckstein. This combination included Consolidated Goldfields and S. Neumann & Co. Professor John Atkinson Hobson writes in *The War in South Africa Its Causes and Effects* that "Rothschild has a controlling interest in Goetz & Co." and that "Rothschild stands for the Exploration Company which is in effect Wernher, Beit and Rothschild"[77] Furthermore he adds that the dynamite monopoly and "the rich and powerful liquor trade, licit and illicit, is entirely in the hands of the Jews"; "the Stock Exchange, is needless to say, mostly Jewish" and "the press of Johannesburg is chiefly their property".[78]

By the early 1890s the foreign workers and speculators had started to outnumber the Boers. In 1896, after the abortive Jameson Raid, which tried to overthrow the Transvaal government, the South African League was founded as a Rothschild front in order to agitate for the granting of voting rights to the *uitlanders* or foreigners. In order to protect their status the Boers would only grant the franchise after a period of 14 years of residence. On 30 May 1899 at a conference held in Bloemfontein, the capital of the Orange Free State, President Paul Krüger, offered to reduce the period of residence to seven years. The British High Commissioner, Sir Alfred Milner, was unmoved and held to his point of view that it was "reform or war".[79] Eventually, Krüger "bowing his head between his big red hands, hot tears streaming down his bearded cheeks"[80] cried out in anguish "It is my country that you want!"[81]

In September 1899 in an act of provocation, the British started to mass troops on the southern Transvaal border. A request

---

77 *Ibid.*, 193. See also R. Rudman, *England Under The Heel Of The Jew.* This 21 page pamphlet was extracted from the book of the same title written in 1918 by Dr. John Henry Clarke, a physician, and was published by C.F. Roworth in London. It provides a graphic account of the conspiracy by the Jewish Randlords to overthrow the Kruger government.

78 *Ibid.*, 193.

79 P.J Pretorius, *Volksverraad*, Libanon-Uitgewers, Mosselbaai, Western Cape, 1996, 58.

80 R. Kraus, *Old Master Thereof Jan Christian Smuts*, E.P. Dutton & Co. Inc., New York, 1944, 92.

81 T. Pakenham, *The Boer War*, Jonathan Ball Publishers, London, 1979, 68.

on 9 October 1899 that Her Majesty's government cease "the constant bringing up of troops to the borders of the Republic, and the sending of reinforcements from all parts of the British Empire"[82] was ignored. Two days later war broke out. Although the Boers had only a part time army of mounted horsemen, they enjoyed stunning successes in the initial phase of the war. However, they were ultimately outgunned, outnumbered and in some instances poorly led. From June 1900 onwards the Boers resorted to guerrilla warfare. A tiny force of never more than 6,000 active Boers was able to frustrate and tie down almost 450,000 troops of the world's largest empire.

Peace was signed at Vereeniging on 31 May 1902. The war had been an unmitigated disaster for the Boers. In contravention of the Hague Convention of 29 July 1899, which bound Great Britain to observe its "rules of civilised warfare", an unprecedented scorched earth policy was introduced. The Boers' homesteads were razed to the ground, wells were poisoned, their cattle were slaughtered and their women were raped. Twenty-five towns and their contents and 20 villages, including all their churches, were destroyed. 155,000 women and children were herded into 46 concentration camps and housed in tents, where in some camps during winter temperatures fell below zero. 34,000 of them died of malnutrition, poor sanitation and exposure, of whom 81% were under the age of 16. The British also suffered high losses with 21,942 being killed (35% in battle, 65% from disease) and 22,829 being wounded. The bankers had the satisfaction of obtaining full control of the gold and other mineral resources of South Africa, of financing the war in the amount of £222 million and thereby adding a further £132 million[83] to Britain's national debt. For Nathan, Alfred and Leopold Rothschild the Anglo-Boer War was a consummate victory.

---

82   S.M. Goodson, *General Jan Christian Smuts The Debunking of a Myth*, Bienedell Uitgewers, Pretoria, 2013, 11.

83   In 2016 £222 million and £132 million were worth £25 billion and £14.9 billion respectively.

The Commonwealth Bank of Australia

The Commonwealth Bank of Australia was inspired by King O'Malley, an American, who found out the secrets of fractional reserve banking while working for his uncle's bank in New York in the 1880s. When the bank's first governor, Sir Dennison Miller, was asked where he proposed obtaining capital for his bank, he replied, "What capital? I don't need any capital, my capital is the entire wealth and credit of the whole of Australia."[84] With an advance of £10,000 from government, which was quickly repaid, the Commonwealth Bank of Australia was founded on 15 July 1912. Although established as a private bank, it operated as a state bank with the power to carry on all business generally transacted by banks, including that of a savings bank. Furthermore the bank was entitled to raise capital through the sale of debentures secured by the national credit. Its profits were equally divided into two funds – a reserve fund to meet any liabilities incurred by the bank and a redemption fund to redeem debentures or other stock issued by the bank. Thereafter 50% of its profits were allocated for the liquidation of the National Debt.

For the next 12 years, notwithstanding the years of World War I (1914-18), Australia enjoyed one of its greatest eras of prosperity. By providing government loans at a nominal rate of interest viz. ⅔rds of one per centum per annum, it enabled the country to embark on a huge infrastructure programme. It included provision of A$18.72 million for the construction of dams and the Murrumbidgee irrigation system, the great Transcontinental Railroad, electricity power plants, gasworks, harbours, roads and tramways. In addition, the fruit, wheat and wool crops of farmers were financed for an amount of A$3 million at nominal rates of interest. It made available A$4 million to purchase 15 cargo steamers in order to transport Australia's growing exports and A$8 million were allocated to subsidised housing. World War I cost Australia A$700 million, but it was financed by the bank as a non-interest bearing debt.

---

84 R. Gollam, *op.cit.*, provides a detailed background of the events leading up to the bank's establishment.

King O'Malley (1854-1953) who was the inspiration for the founding of Australia's state bank, the Commonwealth Bank of Australia.

This phenomenal period of prosperity was terminated in 1924 when a bill, which placed control of the bank in the hands of a directorate consisting of a Governor, the Secretary to the Treasury and six persons actively engaged in agriculture, finance and industry for different terms of years, was introduced by Stanley Melbourne Bruce, prime minister (1924-29) and Dr. Earle Page his coalition partner.[85] There is a suspicion that Bruce may have been bribed, as what he did was completely against the best interests of the Australian people. During his term of office the Australian government borrowed £230 million from the City of London[86] and by 1927 the federal and state debt had reached £1 billion and the budget was in deficit.[87]

On 10 October 1924 the bill was proclaimed as an Act. The subsequent effect of this Act was to place the bank under the control of a body of men, who later deprived it of the right to create the nation's money supply free of debt and interest. In 1927 the bank lost its savings bank subsidiary, and although it was permitted to continue issuing bank notes and thereby earn

85   Bruce and Earle were the leaders of the National and Country parties respectively.

86   S. McIntyre, *A Concise History of Australia,* Cambridge University Press, Melbourne, 2009, 168.

87   I.M. Cumpston, *Lord Bruce of Melbourne*, Longman Cheshire, Melbourne, 1989, 74.

a modicum of seigniorage, it thereafter became a central bank operating exclusively for the benefit of private banks.

The final betrayal of the bank occurred on 20 March 1947 when the House of Representatives voted by 55 to 5 votes for it to become a member of the International Monetary Fund and thus subject to the decrees and dictates of the Rothschild controlled Bank for International Settlements.

World War I

World War I started on 28 June 1914 when Gavrilo Princip, allegedly of Jewish origin and a member of a terrorist group, the Black Hand, assassinated Archduke Franz Ferdinand, heir to the Austrian throne, and his Czech born wife at Sarajevo, Bosnia Herzegovina. Princip was a collaborator of Leon Trotsky (real name Lev Davidovitsj Bronstein),[88] a Russian Jew who was conspiring with a fellow Jew Vladimir Lenin (named Ulyanov when adopted, real name Zederbaum)[89] to overthrow the

---

88 For the alleged Jewish provenance of Princips see W.G. Simpson, *Which Way Western Man?*, Yeoman Press, New York, 1978, 682 where he cites Léon de Poncins, *Secret Powers Behind Revolution*, Boswell, 1929, 75, who has in turn cited page 46 of the Pharos shorthand report of the assassin's trial. See also J.M. Landowsky, *Red Symphony*, translated by G. Knupffer, 78 pp. www.archive.org/details/RedSymphony, an interrogation by the NKVD (Stalinist Secret Police) of Christian G. Rakovsky (real name Chaim Rakover), where he states that Trotsky was behind the murder of Archduke Ferdinand and that the Soviet five-pointed star represents the five banking branches of the Rothschild brothers (Frankfurt, London, Naples, Paris and Vienna).

89 On his paternal side Lenin's father was a Buryat, a non-ethnic Russian. His maternal great-grandfather was Moishe Itskovich Blank and his grandfather Srul Moisevich Blank. The latter later changed his fore-name to Alexander. Zev Ben-Shlomo, review of Lenin-Life and Legacy, Dmitri Volkogonov, *Jewish Chronicle*, London, 4 April 1995. Lenin's Jewish mother was Maria Blank. When his parents died, he and his brother were adopted by a Jewish family. In 1929 Lenin's sister Anna Ulilanova-Yelizarov proposed to Stalin that his ancestry be disclosed so as to counter rampant anti-Semitism and instill in the masses his "Jewish revolutionary spirit." Notwithstanding the fact that Lenin was allegedly revered by the masses, Stalin told her to keep quiet as disclosure would make everyone realise that the Bolshevik Revolution was 100% Jewish. Jesse Zel Lurie, Lenin was a Secret Jew, *Bronward Jewish Journal*, 25 February 1992. According to a report in *The Times* of 10 May 1920, which was compiled from Soviet Sources, 458 or 82.4% out of a total of 556 principal state functionaries were Jews. The author has visited one of the last remaining Lenin museums in Tampere, Finland, where Lenin planned the November 1905 revolution in Russia.

Automobile pioneer, Henry Ford, identified the international Jewish bankers as being the instigators of World War I, expressing his views in *The International Jew* published by the *Dearborn Independent* newspaper.

Russian monarchy. He was in turn financed by an American Jew Jacob Schiff,[90] who was a front man for an English Jew Lord Nathan Rothschild, who was one of the masterminds behind

90   A.C. Sutton, *op.cit.*, 186-196.

this appalling catastrophe. These facts were confirmed in the United States Senate in 1921, when it was recorded that "Full responsibility for the First World War lies on the shoulders of the International Jewish Bankers. They are responsible for Millions of dead and dying."[91]

In late October 1926 further confirmation of these incontrovertible facts was revealed in a conversation between British parliamentarian Victor H Cazalet and Henry Ford (1863-1947). When the former asked who the international Jewish financiers were, Ford replied: "I have several books which will tell you who they all are. They were responsible for the last war, and will in the future always be capable of creating a war when they feel their pockets need one."[92]

Trade rivalry, competing alliances and misunderstood mobilisations are often proffered as being the primary causes of World War I. However, the real reasons in order of importance are as follows:

1. To destroy the Russian Empire and its State Bank.

2. To break up the other empires (Austro-Hungarian, German and Ottoman) into smaller states, which could then be exploited more efficiently through the establishment of central banks.

3. The theft of Palestine and the creation of a Zionist puppet state under the direct control of the Rothschilds.[93]

91 US Congress Record, 67th Congress, 4th Sitting, Senate Document no. 346, 1921.
In 1928 Jewish writer, Marcus Eli Ravage wrote as follows: "You have not begun to appreciate the real depth of our guilt. We are intruders. We are subverters. We have taken your natural world, your ideals, your destiny, and played havoc with them. We have been at the bottom not merely of the latest Great War [WW I] but of nearly all your wars, not only of the Russian but of every other major revolution in your history. We have brought discord and confusion and frustration into your personal and public life. We are still doing it. No one can tell how long, we shall go on doing it." *The Century Magazine*, January 1928, Vol. 115, No. 3, 346-350, as cited in B. Klassen, *The White Man's Bible, The Church of the Creator*, Otto, North Carolina, 1981, 287-289.

92 A.N. Field, *The Truth About The Slump – What The News Never Tells*, Privately published, Nelson, New Zealand, 1935, 93.

93 N. Ferguson, *The House of Rothschild, The World's Banker 1849-1999*, Vol. 2, Penguin Books, London, 1999, 449.

By the end of 1916 the British and French armies were in danger of losing the war, with the latter army having already mutinied on the Western front. The British had lost their naval supremacy at the Battle of Jutland on 3 May 1916, when the German Navy, outnumbered by two to one, humiliated the invincible Royal Navy, sinking 12 vessels for the loss of six and losing 2,551 sailors compared to the British loss of 6,094.[94] Both Kaisers were desperate to bring an end to this fratricidal and pointless slaughter. Seemingly out of the blue came an offer from Lord Rothschild to secure American intervention in return for handing over Palestine to a group of Jewish Zionists after the liquidation of the Ottoman Empire.[95] On 6 April 1917 the United States declared war on Germany [96] and the other central powers and on 2 November 1917 Lord Rothschild and his Zionist collaborators received their written undertaking by Great Britain to eventually hand over Palestine to Jewish settlers.[97] This infamous document known as the Balfour Declaration, was drafted by Lord Arthur

---

94   L. Degrelle, *Hitler Born At Versailles*, Vol. 1 of the Hitler Century, Institute for Historical Review, Costa Mesa, California, 1998, 38.

95   The Young Turks who engineered the collapse of the Ottoman Empire were mainly *Donmeh* (Turkish for convert) Jews, who secretly followed the Jewish religion of Sabbateanism, which had been founded by Sabbatai Sevi in the mid-seventeenth century. P. Papaherakles, The Young Turks and the Slaughter of 117 Million Whites, *The Barnes Review*, Washington D.C., Vol. XVIII, No. 2, March/April 2012, 22-31.

96   In a speech given at the Willard Hotel, Washington, D.C. in 1961, former Jew and convert to Roman Catholicism, Benjamin Freedman (Friedman) confirmed how the German Jews had betrayed Germany in World War I by tricking the USA into joining England in return for the latter's promise of Palestine. https://youtu.be/aHdXiRKjwJI

97   Over 98% of the Zionist settlers in Palestine are Ashkenazim, who have no ethnic or Semitic connection with the territory whatsoever. They are descendants of the kingdom of Khazaria, which was situated in modern day southern Russia and Georgia, who were subjected to a mass conversion to Judaism by their monarch, King Bulan, in the eighth century AD. Further confirmation may be found in an article on craniometry by Dr. Maurice Fishberg in the *Jewish Encyclopaedia* IV, 1902, 331-335. This study of nearly 3,000 Jewish heads from a wide variety of countries over a 20 year period, revealed that they were brachycephalic or broad-headed with a cephalic index of 80; in contrast to the heads of Arabs, which are dolicephalic or long-headed. See also Arthur Koestler, *The Thirteenth Tribe: The Khazar Empire and its Heritage*, Random House, 1976, 255 pp. and Shlomo Sand, *The Invention of the Jewish People*, Verso, 2009, 344 pp. and *The Invention of the Land of Israel*, Verso, 2012, 304 pp. On 5 December 2012 a treatise, which was written by Dr. Eran Elhaik, a geneticist researcher at Johns Hopkins University School of Medicine, was published by the Oxford University Press on behalf of the Society of Molecular Biology and Evolution and confirmed that the "Khazarian Hypothesis" is scientifically correct.

Foreign Office,

November 2nd, 1917.

Dear Lord Rothschild,

      I have much pleasure in conveying to you, on behalf of His Majesty's Government, the following declaration of sympathy with Jewish Zionist aspirations which has been submitted to, and approved by, the Cabinet

      "His Majesty's Government view with favour the establishment in Palestine of a national home for the Jewish people, and will use their best endeavours to facilitate the achievement of this object, it being clearly understood that nothing shall be done which may prejudice the civil and religious rights of existing non-Jewish communities in Palestine, or the rights and political status enjoyed by Jews in any other country"

      I should be grateful if you would bring this declaration to the knowledge of the Zionist Federation.

[signature]

Letter from Lord Arthur Balfour to Lord Walter Rothschild, the head of the Zionist Federation expressing British support for the establishment of a Zionist state in Palestine.

James Balfour, British Foreign Secretary and General Jan Christian Smuts, a member of the Imperial War Cabinet. The misery of this unnecessary war dragged on for another two years. Russia was totally destroyed and an insoluble problem was created in the Middle East. As Rabbi Reichorn prophetically remarked in 1859, "Wars are the Jews' harvest, for with them, we wipe out the Christians and get control of their gold. We have already killed 100 million of them. We shall drive the Christians into war by exploiting their national vanity and stupidity. They will then massacre each other, thus giving room for our own people."[98] In similar vein Gutle Schnapper, Mayer Amschel Rothschild's wife, is reputed to have said shortly before she died in 1849, "If my sons did not want war, there would have been none."[99]

An armistice was declared on 11 November 1918 and seven months later on 28 June 1919 the deeply flawed Treaty of Versailles was signed. Germany had to accept exclusive blame and pay extortionate reparations of £6.6 billion[100] equivalent to the entire wealth of the country, even though the other principal belligerents England, France and Russia were equally, if not more blameworthy. This indemnity would be used to repay the international bankers the fraudulent loans and interest, which had been previously lent to the governments of Great Britain and France. As General Smuts said at the conference, "Everything we have done here is far worse than the Congress of Vienna. The statesmen of 1815 at least knew what was going on. Our statesmen have no idea."[101]

---

98   *Le Contemporain,* 1 July 1880.

99   N. Ferguson, *op.cit.,* 20.

100 According to the Bank of England's inflation calculator www.bankofengland.co.uk/ education/Pages/inflation/calculator/flash/default.aspx £6.6 billion was worth £313 billion in 2016.

101 L. Degrelle, *op.cit.,* 335.

Chapter V

The Great Depression

"Capital must protect itself in every possible way, both by combination and legislation. Debts must be collected, mortgages foreclosed as rapidly as possible. When, through process of law, the common people lose their homes, they will become more docile and more easily governed through the strong arm of the government applied by a central power of wealth under leading financiers. These truths are well known among our principal men, who are now engaged in forming an imperialism to govern the world. By dividing the voters through the political party system, we can get them to expend their energies in fighting for questions of no importance. It is thus, by discrete action, we can ensure for ourselves that which has been so well planned and so successfully accomplished".

— Montagu Norman,
Governor of the Bank of England, addressing the United States
Bankers' Association, New York, Idaho Leader, 26 August 1924.

By the turn of the twentieth century there were still only 18 central banks – Swedish Riksbank (1668), Bank of England (1694), Banco de Espana (1782), Banque de France (1800),Bank of Finland (1812), De Nederlandsche Bank[1] (1814), Norges Bank (1816), Österreichische Nationalbank (1816), Danmarks Nationalbank (1818), Banco de Portugal (1846), National Bank of Belgium (1850), Bank Indonesia (formerly Java Bank) (1828), German Reichsbank (1876), Bulgarian National Bank (1879), National Bank of Romania (1880), Bank of Japan (1882), National Bank of Serbia (1884) and the Banca d'Italia (1893).

---

1   *De Nederlandsche Bank* was preceded by the *Amsterdamsche Wisselbank* which was founded in 1609 by Dirck van Os, and therefore may be deemed to be the world's first central bank.

In 1922 a conference was held in Genoa from 10 April to 19 May and attended by heads of state, governors of the Bank of England, Banque de France and the Federal Reserve Bank of New York and a host of other international bankers. At this conference it was resolved to set up central banks in all countries where they were not in existence. The governor of the Bank of England, Montagu Norman,[2] insisted that the central banks should be independent of their governments.[3] A.N. Field in *All These Things* summarises this significant occasion as follows:

"Despite the audacity of these proceedings they were entirely successful. The paid economists duly discovered that reserve banks were marvelous scientific improvements, the newspapers joined in the chorus of applause, and the politicians of the various States behaved as so many bellwethers leading the sheep to the slaughterhouse. The fact was entirely overlooked that the financiers are in no sense public servants, but simply the paid agents of the shareholders in a banking company whose interests need not in the least be identical with the national interest".[4]

The Bank for International Settlements

The number of new central banks increased, particularly "after the establishment of the Bank for International Settlements at Basel early in 1930, when central reserve banks (more or less independent of the Governments of the countries in which they were situated) sprang up like mushrooms all over the world, amid a chorus of approval from deluded Governments and people whom these banks were intended to reduce to servitude."[5]

---

2   Montagu Norman, a freemason, was very secretive and often acted in a clandestine manner. When he travelled abroad, he adopted the nom-de-plume Professor Skinner. This was the surname of his Secretary, Ernest Skinner. Throughout his term of office he would never visit a country, which did not have a central bank and would never hold a conversation with a central bank governor in the presence of a foreign minister of finance. R.S. Sayers, *The Bank of England 1891-1944*, Cambridge University Press, Cambridge, 1976, 159-160.

3   A.N. Field, *All These Things*, Omni Publications, Hawthorne, California, 1936, 7.

4   *Ibid.*, 8.

5   D.J. Amos, *The Story of the Commonwealth Bank*, Veritas Publishing Company Pty Ltd,

The original purpose of the BIS was to facilitate German reparations payments in terms of the Treaty of Versailles, but once the artificially contrived Great Depression started to take effect and the National Socialists assumed power in January 1933, all payments ceased and the BIS had to find a new direction, viz. the fostering of monetary cooperation. In reality the BIS guides and directs the centrally-planned global financial system through the central banks of each country, of which 60 are affiliated to it.

The headquarters of the bank are in Basel, Switzerland and they are currently housed in an ugly 18 storey building, which looks like the cooling tower of a power station. It is an unelected, unaccountable central bank of the central bankers, which has complete immunity from national laws and taxation and has its own private police force. Furthermore in terms of rights granted by an agreement with the Swiss Federal Council, all of the bank's archives, documents and electronic data are inviolable at all times and in all places. This agreement dates back to article X of paragraph 2 of The Hague Protocol which was signed on 31 August 1929 and states that "The Bank, its property and assets, and also the deposits of other funds entrusted to it, on the territory of, or dependent on the administration of…shall be immune from any disabilities and from any restrictive measures such as censorship, requisition, seizure or confiscation, in time of peace or war, reprisals, prohibition or restriction of export of gold or currency and other similar interferences, restrictions or prohibitions." Bi-monthly meetings, where the global economy is discussed, are held in absolute secrecy. There is no written agenda, unless one of the statutes of the bank requires revision, and minutes are not kept. The principal functions of the bank are ostensibly:

1. Facilitating collaboration amongst central banks by means of accords.
2. Promoting financial stability.
3. Research on policy issues.

Leabhariaiiiia i .iiiie Gail

Bullsbrook, Australia, 1986, 27.

4. Acting as a counter party for central banks in their financial transactions.
5. Serving as an agent or trustee in connection with international financial operations.

However, the true nature of the BIS was revealed in the book *Tragedy and Hope* written by insider, Professor Carroll Quigley of Georgetown University, who wrote as follows:

"In addition to these pragmatic goals, the powers of financial capitalism had another far-reaching aim, nothing less than to create a world system of financial control in private hands able to dominate the political system of each country and the economy of the world as a whole. This system was to be controlled in a feudalist fashion by the central banks of the world acting in concert, by secret agreements arrived at in frequent private meetings and conferences. The apex of the system was to be the Bank for International Settlements in Basle, Switzerland, a private bank owned and controlled by the world's central banks which were themselves private corporations. Each central bank, in the hands of men like Montagu Norman of the Bank of England, Benjamin Strong of the New York Federal Reserve Bank, Charles Rist of the Bank of France, and Hjalmar Schacht of the Reichsbank, sought to dominate its government by its ability to control Treasury loans, to manipulate foreign exchanges, to influence the level of economic activity in the country, and to influence cooperative politicians by subsequent economic rewards in the business world."[6]

As Professor Quigley predicted back in 1966, the ultimate aim of the BIS is a single world currency, a one world economic system and a global government, where national laws are no longer applicable or relevant. Control of the bank lies with the House of Rothschild through its investments in various central and private banks.

---

6   C. Quigley, *Tragedy and Hope A History of the World in Our Time*, The Macmillan Company, New York, 1966, 324.

After World War II and the dissolution of the European colonial empires because they were they were no longer financially sustainable and offered far greater prospects for exploitation and plunder by means of international loans,[7] there was a further proliferation of central banks and currently their number stands at 157. Eight of these banks are in private ownership: National Bank of Belgium, Bank of Greece, Banca d'Italia, Bank of Japan, South African Reserve Bank, Swiss National Bank, Central Bank of the Republic of Turkey and the United States Federal Reserve Bank. The co-ordinated establishment of all these central banks proves beyond doubt that they are "part of an international money trust."[8]

United States Federal Reserve Bank

Between 1820 and 1910, although there was a temporary spike in prices during the American Civil War (1861-1865), the dollar retained its purchasing power, viz. one dollar was still worth a dollar 90 years later. However, it took a mere six years for the US Federal Reserve Bank to destroy the value of the dollar. Between 1914 and 1920 prices rose by 125% reducing its value by 56.1%.

Before casting our attention to the Great Depression, a brief examination of the causes of the first major deflation needs to be considered. In order to rein in prices a secret bankers' meeting was held on 18 May 1920 in Washington D.C. under the misleading title of The Orderly Deflation Committee of the American Bankers Association.[9] Under orders of the Federal Reserve Board without notice or warning the discount rate rose rapidly from 2% to 9% and beyond. Simultaneously the Federal

---

7   For insights as to how the World Bank and IMF, in particular through the latter's structural adjustments programmes, have exploited developing countries with foreign loans see P.T. Bauer, *Equality, the Third World, and Economic Delusion*, Harvard University Press, Cambridge, Massachusetts, 1981, 304 pp. and J. Perkins, *Confessions of an Economic Hitman*, Plume, New York, 2005, 303 pp.

8   A.N. Field, *op.cit.*, 5.

9   G.M. Coogan, *Money Creators, Who Creates Money? Who Should Create It?*, Omni Publications, Hawthorne, California, 1963, (first published in 1935), 62.

Reserve Bank began aggressively to sell government bonds, reducing their value by 20%. The fall in bond prices reduced the value of the reserves of the community banks, which were forced to call in all their loans. This resulted in "a terrific liquidation of all agricultural products"[10] and "agricultural prices tumbled to ruinously low levels."[11]

At the same time freight companies, owned by the major trusts such as the Harrimans, increased their railroad rates to such an extent that in some states freight costs exceeded the cost of farm production. The farm product index dropped by more than half from 244 in May 1920 to 117 a year later. Many farmers were ruined as their overheads remained unchanged and their financial costs soared. The unlimited powers which the Federal Reserve Bank possessed had enabled it to contract the currency and credit of the United States by $2 billion with the result that "prices were cut in half and confusion and distress reigned."[12] This policy was carried out with deliberate intent[13] in order to impoverish the agricultural sector[14] by transferring rural money to the urban centres and at the same time reducing America's food independence, thereby making it vulnerable to the intrigues and whims of financial speculators and swindlers.[15]

In July 1921 the Federal Reserve Bank reversed this policy by repurchasing government bonds. However, the damage done to agricultural banks could not be repaired, and agricultural products remained artificially depressed with some products being sold below cost of production.

---

10   *Ibid.*, 62.

11   *Ibid.*, 62.

12   A.N. Field, *The Truth About The Slump*, Self published, Nelson, New Zealand, 1935, 197.

13   *Ibid.*, 200.

14   The deliberate collapse of the American agricultural sector may be compared to the destruction of agricultural production in the 1930s in the Ukraine (Russian for borderland) by Stalin and the subsequent Holodomor (Russian for death by starvation) in which an estimated six million Kulaks (Russian for fist) were either executed or died of hunger.

15   A.N. Field, *op.cit.*, 204.

In August 1927 the conspirators running the privately owned Federal Reserve Bank decided that it was time to create a new "boom". Despite the protestations of 11 of the 12 Federal Reserve Banks, who perceived the danger, they were ordered to lower their rediscount rates and embark on a massive government bond repurchasing programme (the modern equivalent of quantitative easing) to boost the money supply.[16]

Hardly any of this newly created money *ex nihilo* went into productive investments, but was poured into the stock market, where the price/earnings ratio[17] quickly rose to 20 and in some cases to 50. The news media and deluded "economists" announced the arrival of a "new era" of permanent prosperity and purposefully fanned the flames of speculation, as 16 million Americans out of an adult population of 73 million bought and sold shares.

On 9 March 1929 Paul Warburg, freemason and founder of the Federal Reserve Bank, advised all member banks, as well as Secretary of the Treasury and fellow mason, Andrew Mellon, to get out of the stock market or sell it short. He informed them that if they acted immediately, they would reap enormous profits as the Dow Jones share index was about to collapse in a titanic plunge.

On 24 October 1929 the Federal Reserve Bank decided to put an end to this orgy of speculation and to commence the fleecing of the people. The rediscount rate was suddenly increased to 6%. From nowhere thousands of orders arrived at the New York Stock Exchange to sell "at market", a typical stratagem employed by speculators to knock down share prices rapidly. Confidence soon evaporated and the first intentionally planned Great Depression was in full swing. The decisive point came six days later on 30 October 1929 when the Federal Reserve Bank ordered the contraction of brokers' loans in the amount of $2.3 million. The

---

16   G.M. Coogan, *op.cit.*, 67.
17   Ratio is calculated by dividing the share price by the earnings per share.

stock exchange went into a tailspin and by December 1932 the value of its listed securities had fallen by 83.1% from $89 billion to $15 billion.

The economic and social consequences of this implosion were devastating. Out of 24,000 banks, 10,000 were crushed out of existence leaving their depositors ruined. 200,000 companies filed for bankruptcy and 8.3 million people were thrown on to the streets. Within three years 24.9%[18] of the working population was unemployed. The total National Income of the United States declined by 40.7% from $81 billion in 1927 to $48 billion in 1932. During the depression years an estimated three million people died of starvation. The main causes were malnutrition, infectious diseases, starvation and suicide.

When referring to the New York Stock Exchange collapse, which initiated the depression, Congressman Louis T. McFadden stated with precision "It was a carefully contrived occurrence… The international bankers[19] sought to bring about a condition of despair so that they might emerge as the rulers of us all."[20]

A.N. Field condemned the worthlessness of central banks and the perverted purposes for which they have been consistently utilised as follows.

"Reserve banking as a means of preventing financial crises has thus been a most complete and total failure in the United States. This fact has in no way militated against a world campaign to establish reserve banks in all countries. It has been alleged that the financiers in command of the United States Federal Reserve do not want stable conditions, and that the unprecedented booms and slumps since its establishment have been deliberately caused. It is at least certain that those

18   League of Nations, *World Economic Survey: Eighth Year, 1938/9*, (Geneva 1939), 128.
19   During the 1920s and 1930s the term international bankers was a commonly used code word for Jewish bankers. Cosmopolitan financiers was another euphemism employed.
20   A.N. Field, *op.cit.*, 202.

in control of the system have raised the strongest objections to every one of the numerous attempts made in Congress to write an instruction into the law directing the Federal Reserve to use its tremendous powers to maintain the purchasing power of its money at a stable level."[21]

In a newspaper article in the *Financial Times* written in 1930, Professor Karl Gustav Cassel[22] of Stockholm University, Sweden remarked: "Practically absolute power over the welfare of the world has been placed in the hands of the Federal Reserve Board. And one is appalled to see the apparently haphazard manner in which the Board uses this power, how ignorant it is of the aim which ought to dictate American monetary policy."[23]

Finally in this section we may pause to reflect on a thunderous speech given on Friday, 10 June 1932 in the United States House of Representatives by the former chairman of the House Banking and Currency Committee (1920-1931) the Honorable Louis T. McFadden.[24]

"Mr. Chairman, we have in this country one of the most corrupt institutions the world has ever known. I refer to the Federal Reserve Board and the Federal Reserve Banks.

The Federal Reserve Board, a Government board, has cheated the Government of the United States and the people of the United States out of enough money to pay the national debt. The depredations and the iniquities of the Federal Reserve Board and the Federal Reserve Banks acting together have cost this country enough money to pay the national debt

21 A.N. Field, *All These Things*, Omni Publications, Hawthorne, California, 1936, 121-122.
22 Professor Cassel was a founding member of the *Handelshögskolen i Stockholm* (Stockholm School of Economics). The school was fundamentally opposed to the gold standard propagated by the Austrian School of Economics.
23 A.N. Field, *The Truth About The Slump*, 118.
24 '*Collective Speeches of Congressman Louis T. McFadden*', Omni Publications, Hawthorne, California, 1970, Chap. XVI, The Treacherous and Disloyal Conduct of the Federal Reserve Board and the Federal Reserve Banks, 298-329.

several times over. This evil institution has impoverished and ruined the people of the United States; has bankrupted itself, and has practically bankrupted our Government. It has done this through the defects of the law under which it operates, through the maladministration of that law by the Federal Reserve Board, and through the corrupt practices of the moneyed vultures who control it.

Some people think the Federal Reserve Banks are United States Government institutions. They are not Government institutions. They are private credit monopolies which prey upon the people of the United States for the benefit of themselves and their foreign customers; foreign and domestic speculators and swindlers; and rich and predatory money lenders. In that dark crew of financial pirates there are those who would cut a man's throat to get a dollar out of his pocket; there are those who send money into the States to buy votes to control our legislation; and there are those who maintain international propaganda for the purpose of deceiving us and of wheedling us into the granting of new concessions which will permit them to cover up their past misdeeds and set again in motion their gigantic train of crime.

Those 12 private credit monopolies were deceitfully and disloyally foisted upon this country by bankers who came here from Europe and who repaid us for our hospitality by undermining our American institutions. Those bankers took money out of this country to finance Japan in a war against Russia. They created a reign of terror in Russia with our money in order to help that war along, instigated the separate peace between Germany and Russia and thus drove a wedge between the allies in the World War. They financed Trotsky's mass meetings of discontent and rebellion in New York. They paid Trotsky's passage from New York to Russia, so that he might assist in the destruction of the Russian Empire. They fomented and instigated the Russian Revolution and they placed a large fund of American dollars at Trotsky's disposal in one of their branch banks in Sweden so that through him Russian homes might be thoroughly broken up and Russian children flung far and wide from their natural protectors. They have since begun the breaking up of American homes and the dispersal of American children.

It has been said that President Wilson was deceived by the attentions of these bankers and by the philanthropic poses they assumed. It has been said that when he discovered the manner in which he had been misled by Colonel House, he turned against that busybody, that "holy monk" of the financial empire, and showed him the door. He had the grace to do that, and in my opinion he deserves great credit for it.

President Wilson died a victim of deception. When he came to the Presidency, he had certain qualities of mind and heart which entitled him to a high place in the councils of this nation; but there was one thing he was not and which he never aspired to be; he was not a banker. He said that he knew very little about banking. It was, therefore, on the advice of others that the iniquitous Federal Reserve Act, the death warrant of American liberty, became law in his administration.

Mr. Chairman, there should be no partisanship in matters concerning the banking and currency affairs of this country, and I do not speak with any.

In 1912 the National Monetary Association, under the chairmanship of the late Senator Nelson W. Aldrich, made a report and presented a vicious bill called the National Reserve Association Bill. This bill is usually spoken of as the Aldrich bill. Senator Aldrich did not write the Aldrich bill. He was the tool, but not the accomplice, of the European-born [Jewish] bankers who for nearly 20 years had been scheming to set up a central bank in this country and who in 1912 had spent and were continuing to spend vast sums of money to accomplish their purpose.

The Aldrich bill was condemned in the platform upon which Theodore Roosevelt was nominated in the year 1912, and in that same year, when Woodrow Wilson was nominated, the Democratic platform, as adopted at the Biltmore convention, expressly stated: "We are opposed to the Aldrich plan or a central bank." This was plain language. The men who ruled the Democratic Party then promised the people that if they were returned to power there would be no central bank established here while they held the reins of government. Thirteen months later that promise was broken, and the Wilson administration, under the tutelage of those sinister Wall Street figures who stood behind Colonel House, established here in our free country the worm-eaten monarchial institution of the "king's bank" to control us from the top downward, and to shackle us from the cradle to the grave. The Federal Reserve Act destroyed our old and characteristic way of doing business; it discriminated against our 1-name commercial paper[25], the finest in the world; it set up the antiquated 2-name paper[26], which is the present curse of this country, and which has wrecked every country which has ever given it scope; it fastened down upon this country the very tyranny from which the framers of the Constitution sought to save us.

One of the greatest battles for the preservation of this Republic was fought out here in Jackson's day, when the Second Bank of the United States, which was founded upon the same false principles as those which are exemplified in the Federal Reserve Act, was hurled out of existence. After the downfall of the Second Bank of the United States in 1837, the country was warned against the dangers that might ensue if the predatory interests, after being cast out, should come back in disguise and unite themselves to the Executive, and through him acquire control of the government. That is what the predatory interests did when they came back in the livery of hypocrisy and under false pretences obtained the passage of the Federal Reserve Act.

---

25   A commercial paper such as a cheque or promissory note that has only one signatory.

26   A commercial paper signed by two persons both of whom accept full liability.

The danger that the country was warned against came upon us and is shown in the long train of horrors attendant upon the affairs of the traitorous and dishonest Federal Reserve Board and the Federal Reserve Banks. Look around you when you leave this chamber and you will see evidences of it on all sides. This is an era of economic misery and for the conditions that caused that misery, the Federal Reserve Board and the Federal Reserve Banks are fully liable. This is an era of financed crime and in the financing of crime, the Federal Reserve Board does not play the part of a disinterested spectator.

The people of the United States are being greatly wronged. If they are not, then I do not know what "wronging the people" means. They have been driven from their employments. They have been dispossessed of their homes. They have been evicted from their rented quarters. They have lost their children. They have been left to suffer and to die for the lack of shelter, food, clothing and medicine.

The wealth of the United States and the working capital of the United States has been taken away from them and has either been locked in the vaults of certain banks and great corporations or exported to foreign countries for the benefit of the foreign customers of those banks and corporations. So far as the people of the United States are concerned, the cupboard is bare. It is true that the warehouses and coal yards and grain elevators are full, but the warehouses and coal yards and grain elevators are padlocked and the great banks and corporations hold the keys.

The sack of the United States by the Federal Reserve Board and Federal Reserve Banks and their confederates is the greatest crime in history.

Mr. Chairman, a serious situation confronts the House of Representatives today. We are the trustees of the people and the rights of the people are being taken away from them.

Through the Federal Reserve Board and the Federal Reserve Banks, the people are losing the rights guaranteed to them by the Constitution. Their property has been taken from them without due process of law. Mr. Chairman, common decency requires us to examine the public accounts of the Government to see what crimes against the public welfare have been or are being committed.

What is needed here is a return to the Constitution of the United States. We need to have a complete divorce of Bank and State. The old struggle that was fought out here in Jackson's day must be fought over again. The Independent United States Treasury should be re-established and the Government should keep its own money under lock and key in the building the people provided for that purpose. Asset currency, the device of the swindler, should be done away with.

The Government should buy gold and issue United States currency on it. The business of the independent bankers should be restored to them. The State banking systems should be freed from coercion. The Federal Reserve districts should be abolished and state boundaries should be respected. Bank reserves should be kept within the borders of the States whose people own them, and this reserve money of the people should be protected so that international bankers and acceptance bankers and discount dealers cannot draw it away from them. The exchanges should be closed while we are putting our financial affairs in order. The Federal Reserve Act and the Federal Reserve Banks, having violated their charters should be liquidated immediately.

Faithless Government officers who have violated their oaths of office should be impeached and brought to trial. Unless this is done by us, I predict that the American people, outraged, robbed, pillaged, insulted, and betrayed as they are in their own land, will rise in their wrath and send a President here who will sweep the money changers out of the temple."

U.S. Congressman Louis Thomas McFadden served as Chairman of the United States House Committee on Banking (1920-1931). His persistent exposure of the US Federal Reserve Bank's "gigantic train of crime" led to his assassination on 1 October 1936.

From the above speech, it may be noted that the concerns raised by the Labour Party in South Africa, during the debate on the South African Banking and Currency Bill, that "what had been done in the USA was not in the interests of the public but of the banks"[27] were fully justified. That the naïve and foolish legislators of 1920 allowed the South African Reserve Bank to be established as a replication of the US Federal Reserve Bank, which Congressman McFadden described as being "one of the most corrupt and evil institutions in the world", is a matter of deep regret and must be censured in the strongest terms.

Clifford Hugh Douglas

Clifford Hugh Douglas (1879-1952) was an engineer who, while working as Assistant Superintendent at the Royal Aircraft Factory at Farnborough, England during World War I, noticed that the total costs of goods were greater than the sums paid in lieu of wages, salaries and dividends. He decided to investigate this disconnect in the way money flowed through industry, and after collecting data from hundreds of companies found that there was a persistent deficit in purchasing power of consumers relative to total costs of production. He considered income tax to be a negative dividend and instead proposed the payment of a national dividend to all citizens, which would bridge the gap between earnings and prices. This dividend would provide consumers with the additional buying power necessary to absorb all the current production of goods in a non-inflationary manner. This forms part of Douglas's A + B theorem, viz. that prices are always being generated at a faster rate than incomes are produced, so that the total prices of all goods in the economy at any particular stage exceed the total buying power of consumers. Douglas's economic theory known as Social Credit[28] advocated the transfer of the

---

27   *Cape Times*, 28 July 1920.

28   In a letter to H.S. (Jim) Ede dated 5 April 1935, Lawrence of Arabia expressed his opinion on the Douglas credit scheme, contained in Maurice Colbourne's *Economic Nationalism*, as follows: "Economics are like tides. We fail to harness them, yet they ebb and flow. The right thing would be to chart them, but nobody can distinguish their moon." *The Letters of T.E. Lawrence* edited by D. Garnett, Jonathan Cape,

C.H. Douglas. His proposals for social credit and state banking were accepted by the governments of Alberta, Canada and the Empire of Japan.

Prosperity certificate issued by Social Credit Party, Alberta,1936.

money creation process from private banks, which create money out of nothing as an interest-bearing debt, to a state bank.

He also proposed a price adjustment mechanism called the Just Price. This mechanism would reduce prices by a percentage, as a consequence of physical efficiencies introduced into the production process through improvements in technology. In this manner the benefits of technology would flow directly to the workers and increase their standard of living. Douglas was very aware of the fact that these increasing technological advances would make the attainment of full employment an impossibility. [29] Hence his insistence on the payment of a national dividend, which was calculated by adding to a basic income the increase in national production and consumption data.

After World War I Douglas devoted the rest of his life to the promotion of his ideas and gave lectures in many countries, including Australia, Canada, Japan, New Zealand and Norway. He achieved two notable successes.

1. The Social Credit Party obtained control of the provincial government of Alberta, Canada in 1935.

London, 1938, 866.

29   See Appendix II.

2. After a lecture tour in Japan in 1929, his policies were adopted by the Japanese government in 1932.

Douglas's policies were much feared by the international bankers, and in the 1930s they put up a very considerable sum of £5 million[30] in order to counter his highly successful programme of public enlightenment. Douglas had nothing but disdain for central banking and on one occasion while delivering a speech in Newcastle-upon-Tyne in 1937, he described the Bank of England as being a "mental institution."[31]

Irving Norton Fisher

Irving Fisher (1867-1947) was a famous professor of economics at Yale University, who adopted a mathematical approach to resolving economic problems. He is well known for his utility theory, which juxtaposed the measurability of the utility function to demand theory. In his treatise, *The Theory of Interest*, he observed the changes in the value of goods relative to changes in time and interest rates. This later became known as the Quantity Theory of Money. Throughout his life he was active in the eugenics movement.

In March 1913 Senator Robert L. Owen, chairman of the Senate Banking Committee, tried to introduce an alternative bill to the fraudulent Rothschild/Rockefeller[32] banking and currency proposal. The bill would have allowed for the inclusion of staple commodities as part of the monetary base, in addition to gold and silver and would thereby have prevented the possibility of

---

30 According to the Bank of England's Inflation Calculator £5 million was worth £326 million in 2016.

31 C.H. Douglas, *Security Institutional and Personal*, An address delivered in the City Hall, Newcastle-upon-Tyne 9 March 1937, 6. Ezra Pound speaking on Rome Radio on 1 June 1943 characterised the Bank of England as being the "*Stank of England.*"

32 The Rockefellers are descendants of German, possibly Jewish immigrants, who originally spelt their name Roggenfelder. During the Middle Ages, because Jews were not considered to be part of the general citizenship, they were compelled by the German princes to include the suffix of an inanimate object in their surnames. Hence -berg (mountain), -stein (stone) etc.

either inflation or deflation, and would have created true freedom of employment. Irving Fisher assisted Owen in the drafting of this bill, but was subsequently blackmailed into withdrawing his support.

The following illuminating paragraph extracted from Emmanuel Josephson's *The "Federal" Reserve Conspiracy & Rockefellers "Their Gold Corner"* describes what transpired.

"The conspirators determined to block the adoption of the Owen bill. They had Prof. Fisher summoned before the Yale officials and confronted with the charge that he was so 'foolish' as to advocate money based on commodities other than gold. He was warned, related Sen. Owen, that there would be no place at Yale, or in any other university, for anyone so 'foolish'. Prof. Fisher was keenly aware of the side on which 'his bread was buttered'; and was no more principled, unfortunately, than are the multitude of 'professors' prostituted to the conspirators and their foundations. He succumbed to the conspirators' blackmail, double crossed Sen. Owen and withdrew his professorial support of the honest remedial bill that he had helped draft. In its place, Prof. Fisher announced his advocacy of what he mockingly labeled a 'commodity' dollar the value of which was to be determined by a 'gold index', that would block stabilisation of the economy by making speculative the value of commodities, of gold and of the dollar, and would enhance the power of the conspirators to manipulate, or 'manage', the economy to enable them more readily to swindle the nation. The *coup de grace* was given to Sen. Owen's honest, stabilizing currency and banking bill by its flat and categoric rejection by Pres. Wilson."[33]

Having relented after his previous betrayal of Senator Owen's

---

[33]   E.M. Josephson, *The "Federal" Reserve Conspiracy & Rockefellers, Their "Gold Corner"*, Chedney Press, New York, 1968, 51.

WORLD'S HIGHEST STANDARD OF LIVING

There's no way like the American Way

Illusion and reality - unemployment line Chicago 1937.

efforts to amend the Currency and Banking Bill, in 1920 Fisher published a book *Dollar Stabilisation*,[34] which contained what later became known as the Chicago Plan.[35] The plan was privately issued as a six page memorandum and distributed to 40 individuals on 16 March 1933. It advocated that the state should create the nation's money supply and that private banks should operate as full reserve banks. Using mathematical principles, Fisher was able to prove that full employment would be the result, business cycles would be abolished and inflation would be reduced and remain at zero.

In August 2012 two researchers at the International Monetary Fund, Jaromir Benes and Michael Kumhoff produced *The Chicago Plan Revisited*. They found that every one of Fisher's findings was 100% correct. Their conclusion is cited in full.

---

34 A.N. Field, *op.cit.*, 169.

35 Fisher was aware of the advantages of money issued publicly, free of debt and interest, at the local level in Europe. In *Stamp Scrip*, Adelphi Publishers, New York, 1933, he devotes Chapter IV to The First Experiments Abroad: Silvio Gesell. Gesell introduced the Wara (*Ware und Währung* – Goods and Currency) paper money successfully into the depressed coal mining town of Schwanenkirchen, Bavaria. In Chapter V: The Sudden Spread of 'Scrip' he describes how stamp scrip transformed the depressed town of Wörgl, Austria into a flourishing centre of prosperity.

Professor Irving Fisher's Chicago Plan of 1933, which proposed full reserve banking, was endorsed by researchers from the International Monetary Fund in 2012.

"This paper revisits the Chicago Plan, a proposal for fundamental monetary reform that was put forward by many leading U.S. economists at the height of the Great Depression. Fisher (1936), in his brilliant summary of the Chicago Plan, claimed that it had four major advantages, ranging from greater macroeconomic stability to much lower debt levels throughout the economy. In this paper we are able rigorously to evaluate his claims, by applying the recommendations of the Chicago Plan to a state-of-the-art monetary DSGE[36] model that contains a fully micro-funded and carefully calibrated model of the current U.S. financial system. The critical feature

---

36   Dynamic Stochastic General Equilibrium.

of this model is that the economy's money supply is created by banks, through debt, rather than being created debt-free by the government.

"Our analytical and simulation results fully validate Fisher's (1936) claims. The Chicago Plan could significantly reduce business cycle volatility caused by rapid changes in banks' attitude towards credit risk, it would eliminate bank runs, and it would lead to an instantaneous and large reduction in the levels of both government and private debt. It would accomplish the latter by making government-issued money, which represents equity in the commonwealth rather than debt, the central liquid asset of the economy, while banks concentrate on their strength, the extension of credit to investment projects that require monitoring and risk management expertise. We find that the advantages of the Chicago Plan go even beyond those claimed by Fisher.

One additional advantage is large steady state output gains due to the removal or reduction of multiple distortions, including interest rate risk spreads, distortionary taxes, and costly monitoring of macro-economically unnecessary risks. Another advantage is the ability to drive steady state inflation to zero in an environment where liquidity traps do not exist, and where monetarism becomes feasible and desirable because the government does in fact control broad monetary aggregates. This ability to generate and live with zero steady state inflation is an important result, because it answers the somewhat confused claim of opponents of an exclusive government monopoly on money issuance, namely that such a monetary system would be highly inflationary. There is nothing in our theoretical framework to support this claim. And as discussed in Section II, there is very little in the monetary history of ancient societies and Western nations to support it either."[37]

---

[37]   IMF working paper, August 2012. https://www.imf.org/external/pubs/ft/wp/2012/wp12202.pdf

Chapter VI

The Rise and Fall of State Banking (1932-1945)

"You are aware that the gold standard has been the ruin of the States which adopted it, for it has not been able to satisfy the demands for money, the more so that we have removed gold from circulation as far as possible".

– Protocol No. 20 [1]

"I next argued that the gold standard, the fixing of rates of exchange and so forth were shibboleths which I had never regarded and never would regard as weighty and immutable principles of economy. Money, to me, was simply a token of exchange for work done, and its value depended absolutely on the value of the work accomplished. Where money did not represent services rendered, I insisted, it had no value at all".

– Adolf Hitler [2]

Reichsbank: The State Bank of National Socialist Germany

Out of the world-wide chaos and economic havoc of the 1930s, which had been induced by the Rothschild controlled/owned central banks, three phoenixes would arise.

In May 1919 an insignificant soldier attended a lecture given by a former construction engineer turned economist, Dr. Gottfried

---

1   *The Protocols of the Meetings of the Learned Elders of Zion*, translated from the Russian text by Victor E. Marsden, former Russian correspondent of *The Morning Post*, London, 1934, 214. (Victor Marsden was the public relations officer of HRH The Prince of Wales on his Empire tour of 1920).

2   *Hitler's Table Talk*, compiled by M. Bormann, Ostera Publications, 2012, 311.

Feder (1883-1941) entitled *The Abolition of Interest Servitude*.[3] The purpose of this course of lectures was to provide the soldiers with a background in politics and economics, which would enable them to monitor the many revolutionary and political movements active in Munich at that time. The following quotations taken from *Mein Kampf*[4] reveal the decisive influence that Feder would have on Adolf Hitler's thinking.

"For the first time in my life I heard a discussion which dealt with the principles of stock exchange capital and capital which was used for loan activities. After hearing the first lecture delivered by Feder, the idea immediately came into my head that I had found a way to one of the most essential prerequisites for the founding of a new party.

"To my mind, Feder's merit consisted in the ruthless and trenchant way in which he described the double character of the capital engaged in stock exchange and loan transactions, laying bare the fact that this capital is ever and always dependent on the payment of interest. In the fundamental questions his statements were so full of common sense that those who criticized him did not deny *au fond* that his ideas were sound, but they doubted whether it be possible to put these ideas into practice. To me this seemed the strongest point in Feder's teaching, though others considered it a weak point."[5]

And again,

"I understood immediately that here was a truth of

3 In 1917 Feder formed an organisation called the *Deutscher Kampfbund gegen Zinsknechtschaft* (German Fighting League for the Breaking of Interest Slavery). In 1919 he published his manifesto in the chapter titled *An Alle, Alle! Das Manifest zur Brechung der Zinsknechtschaft* (To Everyone, Everyone! The Manifesto for the Abolition of Interest Slavery) in his book *Kampf gegen die Hochfinanz* (The Struggle against High Finance). https://archive.org/details/Feder-Gottfried-Kampf-gegen-die-Hochfinanz

4 A. Hitler, *Mein Kampf*, Hurst and Blackett, London, 1939, 122.

5 *Ibid.*, 124.

Gottfried Feder (1883-1941). He drafted all the NSDAP's financial policies, but later fell out with Hitler over his lack of support for the latter's synthetic oil from coal project.

transcendental importance for the future of the German people. The absolute separation of stock exchange capital from the economic life of the nation would make it possible to oppose the process of internationalization in German business without at the same time attacking capital as such, for to do this would be to jeopardize the foundations of our national independence. I clearly saw what was developing in Germany, and I realised then that the stiffest fight we would have to wage would not be against the enemy nations but against international capital. In Feder's speech I found an effective rallying-cry for our coming struggle."[6]

A few weeks later Hitler received an instruction from his military superiors to investigate a political association called the *Deutsche Arbeiterpartei* (German Workers Party). At this meeting held on 12 September 1919 in the Sterneckerbrau Inn in Munich, about 20 to 25 persons were present. The main speaker was Gottfried Feder. Shortly thereafter Hitler joined this party and received a provisional certificate of membership numbered seven. His first act on assuming control of the party was to rename it the *Nationalsozialistische Deutsche Arbeiterpartei* (National Socialist German Workers Party).

Feder, who was the principal drafter of the party's 25 points, became the architect and theoretician of the programme. In July 1933 he was appointed Under Secretary of State for Economic Affairs and in 1934 *Reichskommissar* (Reich Commissioner).

Monetary reform was the very essence of National Socialism as is revealed in the following extracts taken from *The Program of the NSDAP, The National Socialist German Workers' Party and its General Conceptions*[7] published in Munich in 1932.

---

6   *Ibid.*, 124.

7   G. Feder, *The Program of the NSDAP, The National Socialist German Workers' Party and its General Conceptions*, translated by E.T.S. Dugdale, Fritz Eher Verlag, Munich, 1932, 51 pp.

Adolf Hitler prints its two main points in leaded type:

The Common Interest Before Self
– The Spirit of the Program

Abolition of the Thralldom of Interest
– The Core of National Socialism.

Once these two points are achieved, it means a victory of their approaching universalist ordering of society in the true state over the present-day separation of state, nation and economics under the corrupting influence of the individualist theory of society as now constructed. The sham state of today, oppressing the working classes and protecting the pirated gains of bankers and stock exchange speculators, is the area for reckless private enrichment and for the lowest political profiteering; it gives no thought to its people, and provides no high moral bond of union. The power of money, most ruthless of all powers, holds absolute control, and exercises corrupting, destroying influence on state, nation, society, morals, drama, literature and on all matters of morality, less easy to estimate.[8]

"Break down the thralldom of interest is our war cry.[9] What do we mean by the thralldom of interest? The landowner is under this thralldom, who has to raise loans to finance his farming operations, loans at such high interest as almost to eat up the results of his labour, or who is forced to make debts and to drag the mortgages after him like so much lead. So is the worker, producing in shops and factories for a pittance, whilst the shareholder draws dividends and bonuses which he has not worked for. So is the earning middle class, whose work goes almost entirely to pay the interest on bank overdrafts.[10]

---

8   *Ibid.*, 21.
9   *Ibid.*, 25.
10   *Ibid.*, 26.

"Thralldom of interest is the real expression for the antagonisms, capital versus labour, blood versus money, creative work versus exploitation. The necessity of breaking this thralldom is of such vast importance for our nation and our race, that on it alone depends our nation's hope of rising up from its shame and slavery; in fact the hope of recovering happiness, prosperity and civilisation throughout the world. It is the pivot on which everything turns; it is far more than mere necessity of financial policy. Whilst its principles and consequences bite deep into political and economic life, it is a leading question for economic study, and thus affects every single individual and demands a decision from each one: Service to the nation or unlimited private enrichment. It means a solution of the Social Question.[11]

"Our financial principle: Finance shall exist for the benefit of the state; the financial magnates shall not form a state within the state. Hence our aim to break the thralldom of interest.

"Relief of the state, and hence of the nation, from its indebtedness to the great financial houses, which lend on interest.

"Nationalisation of the Reichsbank and the issuing houses, which lend on interest.

"Provision of money for all great public objects (waterpower, railroads etc), not by means of loans, but by granting non-interest bearing state bonds and without using ready money.

"Introduction of a fixed standard of currency on a secured basis.

"Creation of a national bank of business development (currency reform) for granting non-interest bearing loans.

---

11   *Ibid.*, 27.

"Fundamental remodelling of the system of taxation on socio-economic principles. Relief of the consumer from the burden of indirect taxation, and of the producer from crippling taxation (fiscal reform and relief from taxation.)[12]

"Wanton printing of bank notes, without creating new values, means inflation. We all lived through it. But the correct conclusion is that an issue of non-interest bearing bonds by the state cannot produce inflation if new values are at the same time created.

"The fact that today great economic enterprises cannot be set on foot without recourse to loans is sheer lunacy. Here is where reasonable use of the state's right to produce money which might produce most beneficial results."[13]

On 30 January 1933 the National Socialists were swept to power[14] by means of a coalition or *Regierung der Nationalen Konzentration* (Government of National Concentration) with the *Deutschnationale Volkspartei* (German National People's Party). A somewhat attenuated version of monetary reform was introduced. In order to finance the state's work and rearmament programmes, two dummy corporations called *Gesellschaft für Offentliche Arbeiten* (Offa) and *Metallforschung Gesellschaft* (Mefo) were established. These corporations accepted bills of exchange from suppliers who fulfilled state orders. These bills of exchange were then discounted at the Reichsbank at a rate of 4%. They were issued for three months only, which was clearly unsatisfactory in view of the long term nature of the various projects they were financing. They could, however, be extended at three monthly intervals for up to five years.

---

12   *Ibid.*, 30.

13   *Ibid.*, 43.

14   In the election of 6 November 1932 the National Socialists obtained 11,737,398 or 33.1% votes. In the election of 5 March 1933 votes received by the NSDAP increased to 17,277,180 or 43.9% of the popular vote. In the election of 12 November 1933 which was in the form of a referendum, the NSDAP received 39,655,224 or 92.1% of the total votes cast in a turnout of 95.3% of all voters.

In January 1939 matters came to a head when the President of the Reichsbank, Hjalmar Schacht, refused extension of three billion Reichsmarks worth of Offa and Mefo bills, because of fears of "inflation". On 7 January 1939 Schacht sent Hitler a memorandum signed by himself and the eight other board members of the Reichsbank, which contained the following main points.

1. The Reich must spend only that amount covered by taxes.

2. Full financial control must be returned to the Ministry of Finance. (Then forced to pay for anything the army desired.)

3. Price and wage control must be rendered effective. The existing mismanagement must be eliminated.

4. The use of money and investment markets must be at the sole discretion of the Reichsbank. (This meant a practical elimination of Göring's Four Year Plan)."[15]

Schacht concluded his memorandum with the ambiguous words: "We shall be happy to do our best to collaborate with all future goals, but for now the time has come to call a halt."[16] By these means Schacht intended to collapse the German economy,[17] which during the period 1933-39 had increased its Gross National Product by 100 percent. From being a ruined and bankrupt nation in January 1933 with 7,500,000 unemployed persons,[18] Hitler had transformed Germany into a modern socialist paradise. He was justifiably angry and rejected the recommendations of the

---

15   E. N. Peterson, *Hjalmar Schacht: for and against Hitler: A political-economic study of Germany, 1923-1945,* The Christopher Publishing House, Boston, 1954, 179.

16   J. Weitz, *Hitler's Banker Hjalmar Horace Greely Schacht,* Little, Brown and Company, London, 1999, 17.

17   *Ibid.,* 343. An indication of where Schacht's true loyalties lay was revealed at his funeral a few days after he had died at the age of 93 on 4 June 1970. One of the wreaths on his coffin had a card, which read "To a companion in hard times – 20 July Foundation." Members of this organisation had unsuccessfully attempted to assassinate Hitler on 20 July 1944.

18   Of the estimated 7,500,000 persons unemployed, 5,575,492 were registered as unemployed, a further 4,000,000 were partially unemployed. *Statistical Year-Book of the League of Nations,* 1940, Geneva, 1940, 70. See also B.R. Mitchell, International Historical Studies, Europe 1750-1993, Fourth edition.

Reichsbank as "mutiny".[19] Two weeks later Schacht was sacked. Roger Elletson describes this momentous event as follows: "On 19 January 1939, Schacht was summarily dismissed, and the Reichsbank was ordered to grant the Reich all credits requested by Hitler. This decisive action essentially emasculated both the Reichsbank's control over domestic monetary policy, and the German power base of international Jewry. It had the effect of removing from Jewish bankers the power to deflate and destroy the German economy.

Excluding the implications of the interest rate paid on the MEFO bills, Germany could now be viewed as being on a "Feder System", rather than a "Schacht System". The Reichsbank effectively became an arm of the government, with the only real change being in the fact that bills were now monetised, or discounted, under the auspices of the State rather than some Jewish lackey in the Reichsbank presidency."[20] Thus only in January 1939 did the Reichsbank become an authentic State Bank. Schacht's dismissal also terminated the transfer of confidential information regarding all Germany's economic developments,[21] which he had been deviously giving without interruption to Montagu Norman,[22] a fellow mason and Governor of the Bank of England (1920-44).

---

19   D. Marsh, *The Bundesbank: The Bank That Rules Europe*, William Heinemann Ltd, London, 1992, 119.

20   R. E. Elletson, *Monetary Parapometrics: A Case Study of the Third Reich*, Christian International Publications, Wilson, Wyoming, 1982, 57.

21   D. Irving, *The War Path: Hitler's Germany 1933-1939*, Macmillan, London, 1978, 172. Footnote: "Montagu Norman, governor of the Bank of England told the U.S. Ambassador Joseph Kennedy that Schacht was his constant informer over 16 years about Germany's precarious financial position (U.S. Ambassador Joseph Kennedy reported this to Washington on 27 February 1939.) In 1946 Norman tried to intercede for Schacht at Nuremberg through a fellow Freemason on the British prosecuting team, Harry Phillimore (Schacht was also a freemason). The U.S. team flatly rejected Phillimore's advances, but the British judge, Birkett successfully voted for an acquittal." See also D. Irving, *Nuremberg The Last Battle*, Focal Point Publishers, London, 1996, 271-272. Montagu Norman was also the godfather of Schacht's youngest grandson, Norman. See Mr. Norman's Visit to Berlin, *The Glasgow Herald*, 5 January 1939, two days before Schacht sent his insolent memorandum to Hitler.

22   Montagu Norman was a surreptitious figure, who adopted a cloak and dagger style of travel and was once seen emerging from the cargo hatch of a freighter. Besides the use of the already mentioned nom-de-plume Professor Skinner, he occasionally used his middle name Collet as his surname.

A new Reichsbank law, which was promulgated on 15 June 1939, made the bank "unconditionally subordinated to the sovereignty of the state."[23]

Article 3 of the law decreed that the bank, renamed the *Deutsche Reichsbank*, should be "directed and managed according to the instructions and under the supervision of the Führer and Reichschancellor."[24]

Hitler was now his own banker, but having departed from the fold of international swindlers and usurers he would, like Napoléon Bonaparte, who in 1800 had established the Banque de France as a state bank, suffer the same fate; an unnecessary war followed by the ruination of his people and country. It was this event which triggered World War II – the realisation by the Rothschilds that universal replication of Germany's usury-free state banking system would permanently destroy their evil financial empire. In order to provide the Poles with a free hand, which would enable them to antagonise and provoke the Germans, a deceitful and worthless offer to guarantee[25] Poland's sovereignty was given by Great Britain on 31 March 1939.

During the next five months the Polish government progressively intensified the oppression, harassment of and attacks on the remaining 1.5 million ethnic Germans living in Poland. These attacks,[26] in which over 58,000 German civilians were killed by

---

23 D. Marsh, *op.cit.*, 128.

24 *Ibid.*, note 40, 300.

25 This was a blank cheque which was guaranteed to bounce, as England was only prepared to come to Poland's aid in the event of a German invasion of Poland or a Polish invasion of Germany, but not one from the Soviet Union. The Poles were unaware of this insidious circumscription. The Soviets annexed by far the larger portion of Poland viz. 77,300 square miles as opposed to the 49,800 square miles restored to Germany. State Secretary Ernst von Weizsäcker cited in D.L. Hoggan, *The Forced War: When Peaceful Revision Failed*, Institute for Historical Review, Costa Mesa, California, 1989, 391, scornfully described "The British guarantee to Poland was like offering sugar to an untrained child before it had learned to listen to reason!"

26 D. L. Hoggan, *op.cit.*, Chap. 16, *The Terrified Germans of Poland*, 388-390 and the Łódź riots 391-392. Hoggan also says that "...there was no doubt among well-informed persons by this time [1939] that horrible atrocities were being inflicted every day on the

Foreign journalists bear witness to murdered Volksdeutscher. Between March and August 1939 the Polish terrorised and murdered tens of thousands of local German civilians, not only in Poland, but also in East Prussia.

Poles in acts of wanton savagery, culminated in the Bromberg massacre on 3 September 1939, in which 5,500 people were murdered. Initially, these provocations and atrocities were stoically ignored. Eventually Hitler was compelled to employ military intervention in order to protect the Germans in Poland. On 30 August 1939, in an act of great statesmanship, Hitler again offered to the Polish government the Marienwerder proposals.[27] The four main proposals were as follows:

1. Retention of the existing 1919 borders as determined by the Treaty of Versailles.
2. The return of Danzig (pop. 370,000) to Germany which was 97% German.
3. Construction of a 60 mile (96 km) autobahn and rail link connecting West and East Prussia, from Schönlanke to Marienwerder.
4. An exchange of German and Polish populations.

Germans of Poland," 554.

27 *Das Letze Angebot in Verheimlichte Dokumente – Was den Deutschen verschwiegen wird* (The Last Offer in Secret Documents – Which are kept hidden from the Germans), Fz-Verlag, Munich, 1993, 172-174. It contains all 16 points.

On the orders of the international bankers, the British Foreign Secretary, Lord Edward Wood Halifax, strongly advised the Polish government not to negotiate.[28] This is how and why World War II was started and disposes of the canard of German culpability. From 1939 onwards, although Germany made at least 28 known attempts at peace without conditions, they were all refused. The ensuing forced war resulted in victory for the international financiers and defeat and slavery for the people of Europe and indeed the world. In Europe this enslavement was finally achieved with the establishment of the Rothschild controlled European Central Bank on 1 June 1998 and the introduction of the euro on 1 January 1999.

Achievements of the German State Banking System

One of the primary benefits which state banking and monetary reform conferred on the German people was the provision of adequate housing. During the period 1933-37 1,458,178 new houses were built to the highest standards of the time.[29] Each house could not be more than two stories high and had to have a garden. The building of apartments was discouraged and rental payments on housing were not permitted to exceed RM25 per month or 1/8 of the income of an average worker. Employees earning higher incomes paid a maximum of RM45 per month.

Interest free loans of RM1,000 (about five months of gross pay) known as *Ehestanddarlehen* (marriage loans) were paid in certificates to newly-wed couples to finance the purchase of household goods. The loan was repayable at 1% per month, but for each child born 25% of the loan was cancelled. Thus if a family had four children, the loan would have been considered repaid in full. The same principle was applied in respect of home loans, which were issued for a period of ten years at a low rate of interest. The birth of each child also resulted in cancellation

---

28   D.L. Hoggan, *op.cit.*, 565-569.

29   From 1932 to 1938 the index for buildings completed rose by 163.2% from 38 to 100.

The People's Car - Adolf Hitler visits the "Volkswagen" factory in Wolfsburg, 1938. The proposed name of the new town was Hitlerstadt, but Hitler demurred preferring his pseudonym Wolf instead.

By September 1939 the Reichsautobahn covered 2,400 miles (3,862 km). It was aesthetically designed to serve not only a utilitarian purpose, but to provide the motorist with scenery and striking views.

of 25% of the loan.[30] Education in schools, technical colleges and universities was free, while the universal health care system provided everyone with free medical care.[31]

During the period 1933-37 imports increased by 31.0% from RM4.2 billion to RM5.5 billion, while exports, particularly to south east Europe, rose by 20.4% from RM4.9 billion to RM5.9 billion. This increased trade is reflected in the 76.9% rise in inland shipping from 73.5 to 130.0 million tons conveyed and the 69.4% rise in ocean shipping from 36 million to 61 million tons transported. During this period trade was greatly enhanced by barter, which bypassed the international payments system and the requirement of having to pay commission and interest on bills of exchange. By the late 1930's 50% of all foreign trade was being conducted by means of barter transactions using offset accounting. There were 25 countries, mainly located in the Balkans and Latin America, participating in such barter agreements. In the same period expenditure on roads and in particular the Reichsautobahn, of which 2,400 miles (3,862km) were completed by September 1939, rose by 229.5% from RM440 million to RM1.45 billion. This construction, which besides having symbolic value representative of the new Germany, was necessary in order to accommodate the substantial increase in licensed vehicles, which rose by 425% from 41,000 to 216,000 vehicles and the even higher increase of 622% in licensed commercial vehicles from 7,000 to 50,600.

Between 1932 and 1938 iron ore production increased by 45.4% from 843,000 to 1,226,000 tons. German ores contained only 25% iron as opposed to the superior iron content of the Swedish ores, which they could not afford. This difficulty was overcome with the Krupp-Renn process which produced high quality steel. Between 1932 and June 1939 the index of coal production rose by 85.5% from 69 to 128, while the energy index rose during the same period by 76.0% from 75 to 132.[32]

---

30   T.L. Stoddard, *Into The Darkness: An Uncensored Report From Inside The Third Reich At War*, Ostara Publications, Burlington Indiana, 1940, 127.

31   The system was funded by modest deductions from workers' wages into the *Allgemeine Ortskrankenkasse* (General Local Health Fund).

32   *Statistical Year-Book of the League of Nations, op.cit.*, 169. Production indices have been

"Wilhelm Gustloff" (25,484 gross tons) named after the leader of the German National Socialists living in Switzerland. As part of the Kraft durch Freude (Strength through Joy) programme, German workers earning less than RM300 a month were able to embark on cruises to exotic destinations. However, these cruise ships were forbidden entry into British ports for fear of creating unrest and envy amongst deprived and unemployed British workers. The Wilhelm Gustloff, while carying Lithuanian, Latvian, and Polish refugee children, sank after being hit by Russian torpedoes on 30 January 1945, with the loss of over 9,000 lives.

Interior of the "Wilhelm Gustloff".

As a result of all this heightened and ever increasing economic activity, unemployment, which stood at 30.1% in 1933, had been reduced to almost zero by July 1939,[33] and retired workers had to be enticed back to the labour market in order to make up for the shortage of skilled workers. In contrast the unemployment rate in the United States, which had stood at 25.1% in 1933, had according to the National Industrial Conference Board declined only marginally to 19.8% by January 1940;[34] a situation which may be attributed to the irrational but nonetheless deliberate policies of the Rothschild controlled Federal Reserve Bank and the parasitic private banking sector.

National income in Germany rose by 43.8% from RM45.2 billion to RM65 billion between 1932 to 1937, while between 1932 and June 1939 the index of producers goods increased by 219.6 % from 46 to 147;[35] yet the cost of living advanced by only 4% or less than 1% per annum, a rate which would be achieved throughout the 12 years of state banking under national socialism. The German monetary policy "was non-inflationary because government expenditures, which increased the level of consumer demand, could in turn elicit a correspondingly increased quantity of disposable consumer goods."[36]

By 1939 Germany had become the most powerful country in the history of Europe. Its Gross Domestic Product at an annual average growth rate of 11% per annum had doubled in the short space of six years of quasi-state banking. The Germans were now the happiest and most prosperous people in the world, fully employed and enjoying one of the highest standards of living. This success was achieved by the hard work of the German people and with the support of an honest money system not based on usury or the gold standard. One of the myths propagated by establishment historians is that Germany's economic renaissance

---

provided by *Konjunkturforschung*, base year 1928.

33   In July 1939 38,379 persons were registered as unemployed.

34   *Statistical Year-Book of the League of Nations, op.cit.,* 70.

35   *Ibid.,* 169.

36   R.E. Elletson, *op.cit.,* 60.

was based on armaments production. The following table reveals modest levels of defence expenditure which only picked up in 1938/1939 when Germany started to feel threatened by her neighbours.

Year	Defence Expenditure RM	National Income
1933/34	1.9 billion	4%
1934/35	1.9 billion	4%
1935/36	4.0 billion	7%
1936/37	5.8 billion	9%
1937/38	8.2 billion	11%
1938/39	18.4 billion	22%

Source: Deutsche Reichsbank

Even expenditure of 22% of national income on defence just before World War II started may be deemed as not being too excessive, when one bears in mind that Germany's borders possess few natural boundaries and at that time she was surrounded by hostile neighbours – Czechoslovakia, France and Poland. Germany also had to replenish the armaments, which she had been forbidden to possess in terms of the Treaty of Versailles. The English historian, A J P Taylor, writes that "The state of German armament in 1939 gives the decisive proof that Hitler was not contemplating general war, and probably not intending war at all."[37]

Post World War II Developments

In May 1945 the *Deutsche Reichsbank* ceased operations, although its affairs were only wrapped up in 1961, and was succeeded in the western half of the country by the *Bank deutscher Länder* (Bank of German States) on 1 March 1948. This bank introduced the Deutsche Mark on 21 June 1948 and later became known as the *Deutsche Bundesbank* which was established on 26 July 1957. Although legally independent and modelled on the US Federal

---

37   A.J.P. Taylor, *The Origins of the Second World War*, Hamish Hamilton, London, 1961, 218.

Reserve Bank, the Bundestag or Federal parliament exerted considerable control and influence over its policies, and it was not as fully independent during that time as most central banks are today.

During 2001 as a result of its membership of the European Central Bank, the *Deutsche Bundesbank* ceded most of its authority to that organisation. Its remaining responsibilities, which are shared with the ECB, are the issuing of bank notes, managing the clearing house, bank supervision and management of currency reserves. The principal objective of the ECB as laid down in Article 127 (1) of the Treaty on the Functioning of the European Union, is to maintain price stability. This obsession is largely responsible for the record levels of unemployment and low levels of growth in GDP currently being experienced, and the ongoing collapse in the birth rate.

The ECB was established on 1 January 1998 and formally became operational on 1 January 1999 with the introduction of the Euro. This Rothschild controlled bank is ironically situated at Kaiserstrasse 29, Frankfurt am Main, not too far from the *Judengasse* (Jews' Lane) where Mayer Amschel Rothschild and his brother Kalman set up a shop peddling coins and medals in the 1780s. For those 18 countries which have foolishly adopted the Euro and joined the ECB, their subjugation and enslavement are a *fait accompli*.

Fascist Italy

On 28 October 1922 Benito Mussolini and his National Fascist Party came to power. Fascism should more appropriately be described as corporatism, as it symbolised a merger of state and corporate power. In 1936 the Chamber of Deputies was replaced by a National Council of Corporations with 823 representatives from industry, labour and the states, who guided industry and settled labour disputes. In the 1920s by means of deficit spending a programme of public works was instituted, which was unrivalled in modern Europe at that time. Bridges, canals, autostrada of 2,485

Mussolini inspects progress on the draining of the Pontine Marshes - one of his engineering triumphs which transformed this region into a thriving agricultural area.

miles (4,000km), hospitals, schools, railway stations and orphanages were built. Forests were planted and universities were endowed.[38] The Pontine marshes were drained and 310 square miles (802 sq.km) were reclaimed.[39] As part of the program of national self-sufficiency or autarky, agriculture was subsidised and regulated.

The State Bank of Italy

In 1926 Mussolini first intervened in the banking sector by granting the Banca d'Italia jurisdiction over the issue of bank notes and the management of minimum requirements for bank reserves, including gold. This formed part of his policy of using Italian fascism "primarily to create an autarkic state not subject to the vagaries of world trade and finance."[40] In 1927 Italy received a loan from JP Morgan of $100 million to meet a special

---

38 R.G. Price, *Fascism Part 1: Understanding Fascism and Anti-Semitism*, 23 October 2003. www.rational/revolution.ne/articles/understanding-fascism.htm

39 Today there are 520,000 inhabitants living in this once deserted region.

40 K. Bolton, *The Banking Swindle Money Creation and the State*, Black House Publishing Ltd, London, 2013, 118.

emergency. Thereafter Mussolini refused "to negotiate or accept any more foreign loans", as "he was determined to keep Italy free from financial subservience to foreign banking interests."[41]

In 1931 the State arrogated to itself the right to supervise all major banks by means of the *Istituto Mobiliare Italiano* (Institute of Italian Securities). In 1936 the process was completed when, by means of the *Atto Reforma Bancaria* (Banking Reform Act), the Banca d'Italia and the major banks became state institutions.[42] The Banca d'Italia was now a fully fledged state bank which had the sole right to create credit out of nothing and advance it for a nominal fee to other banks. Limits on state borrowing were lifted (as was the case with the Bank of Japan see *infra*) and Italy abandoned the gold standard.

The State Bank of Japan

The Bank of Japan or *Nippon Ginkō* was founded on 10 October 1882. Although the Japanese Imperial Household was the largest shareholder, it functioned as a typical central bank, i.e. for the benefit of private banks to the detriment of the public interest.

In 1929 C.H. Douglas, whose system of social credit has been previously discussed, went on a lecture tour of Japan. His proposals for allowing government to create the nation's money and credit free of interest were enthusiastically received by the leaders of both the Japanese government and industry. All Douglas's books and pamphlets were translated into Japanese, and more copies were sold in that country than in the rest of the world.[43]

The reorganisation of the Bank of Japan into a state bank administered exclusively for the accomplishment of national

41 L. Villari, *Italian Foreign Policy under Mussolini*, Holborn Publishing Company, London, 1959, 59.

42 A.J de Grund, *Fascist Italy and Nazi Germany: The 'Fascist' Style of Rule*, George Routledge & Sons Ltd, London, 2004, 52.

43 'New Economics', 19 January 1934, 8 as quoted in D.J. Amos, *The Story of the Commonwealth Bank*, Veritas Publishing Company, Bullsbrook, Western Australia, 1986, 44.

interests was commenced in 1932. The reform of the bank was completed in 1942 when the Bank of Japan Law was remodelled on Germany's Reichsbank Act of January 1939.[44] The bank operated in the following manner:

"It declared that the Bank was a special corporation of a strongly national nature. The Bank was 'to assume the task of controlling currency and finance and supporting and promoting the credit system in conformity with policies of the state to ensure the full use of the nation's potential.' Further, it was 'to be managed with the accomplishment of national aims as its sole guiding principle' (Article 2). As for the functions of the Bank, the law abolished the old principle of priority for commercial finance, empowering it to supervise facilities for industrial finance. The law also authorised the Bank to make unlimited advances to the government without security, and to subscribe for and to absorb government bonds. In respect of note-issues the law made permanent the system of the maximum issues limit; thus, the Bank could make unlimited issues to meet the requirements of munitions industries and of the government. On the other hand, government supervision of the Bank was markedly strengthened. The government could nominate, superintend and give orders to the president and the directors; there was also a clause giving the government more comprehensive powers to give so-called 'functional orders' to the bank, to direct it to perform any function it deemed necessary for the attainment of the Bank's purpose. Moreover, the law made a wide range of the Bank's business subject to governmental approval, including such matters as the alteration of bank rate, note-issues and accounts."[45]

Japan had been experiencing the same traumatic difficulties caused by the artificially created Great Depression. However,

---

44 www.veteranstoday.com/2011/06/26was-world-war-ii-fought-to-make-the-world-safe-for-usury and S.M. Goodson, The Real Reason the Japanese Attacked Pearl Harbor, *The Barnes Review*, Washington D.C., Vol. XIV, No. 6, November/December 2008, 41-45.

45 *Money and Banking in Japan*, the Bank of Japan Economic Research Department, translated by S. Nishimura, edited by L.S. Pressnell, Macmillan, London, 1973, 38.

the conversion from a central to a state banking methodology produced results which were both swift and sustained.

Economic Indices of Japan 1931-41

	Manufacturing	All Industries	National Income	GNP
1931	19.1	19.7	10.5	12.5
1932	20.2	20.8	11.3	13.0
1933	24.7	25.3	12.4	14.3
1934	26.4	27.0	13.1	15.7
1935	27.9	28.7	14.4	16.7
1936	31.5	32.3	15.5	17.8
1937	37.2	37.7	18.6	23.4
1938	38.2	39.0	20.0	26.8
1939	42.4	43.0	25.4	33.1
1940	44.3	44.9	31.0	39.4
1941	45.8	46.5	35.8	44.9

Source: Statistics Department, Bank of Japan

The above table illustrates the progressive improvement which took place in the Japanese economy, once the shackles of usury had been removed. During the 1931-41 period manufacturing output and industrial production increased by 140% and 136% respectively, while national income and Gross National Product were up by 241% and 259% respectively. These remarkable increases exceeded by a wide margin the economic growth of the rest of the industrialised world. In the labour market unemployment declined from 5.5% in 1930 to 3.0% in 1938. Industrial disputes decreased with the number of stoppages down from 998 in 1931 to 159 in 1941.

By the late 1930s Japan had become the leading economic power in East Asia and her exports were steadily replacing those of America and England. In August 1940 Japan announced the formation of the Greater East Asian Co-prosperity Sphere.[46]

---

46 First conceived by General Hachiro Arita, who served in the Ministry of Foreign

Japan's challenge to US and European car manufacturers - The small Datsun automobile was to sell for less than the lowest priced US or UK cars and was in trial order stage for India, Czechoslovakia, and Great Britain. Prince Chichbe, brother to Emperor Hirohito, is shown seated in the car at the Japanese Industrial Association Plant in Yokohama in December 1934.

The fear that these countries would adopt Japan's state banking methods posed such a serious threat to the Rothschild owned and controlled US Federal Reserve Bank, that a war was deemed to be the only means of countering it.

How Japan Was Forced into World War II

From July 1939 relations with America rapidly deteriorated after the USA unilaterally abrogated the Treaty of Commerce of 1911 and thereby restricted Japan's ability to import essential raw materials. These measures were imposed avowedly because of the war in China and were followed in June 1940 by an aviation fuel embargo and a ban on the export of iron and steel to Japan in November 1940. On 25 July 1941 all Japanese assets in England, Holland and America were frozen after Japan, with the

Affairs from 1936 to 1940. It was formally announced by Foreign Minister Matsuoka Yosuke on 1 August 1940.

permission of Vichy France, had peacefully occupied Indochina, in order to block off China's southern supply routes, and all trade between Japan and America was summarily terminated. At the same time President Franklin D. Roosevelt closed the Panama Canal to all Japanese shipping, and a rubber and oil embargo was enforced, which resulted in the latter case, of the loss of 88% of all supplies. Without oil Japan could not survive.

General Hideki Tojo, Prime Minister (October 1941 – July 1944) explains in his diary how the United States continually thwarted Japanese efforts at maintaining peace. Japan's peaceful commercial relations were being persistently undermined by the USA and posed a grave threat to her future existence. By means of the economic blockade a noose was being placed around Japan's neck. Not only were the United States, England, China and Holland encircling Japan through economic pressures, but naval forces throughout the region in the Philippines, Singapore and Malaya were being redeployed and strengthened. American battleships were observed steaming through the seas surrounding Japan. An American admiral claimed that the Japanese fleet could be sunk in a couple of weeks, while British Prime Minister Churchill declared that England would join America's side within 24 hours.

General Tojo wrote: "Japan attempted to circumvent these dangerous circumstances by diplomatic negotiation, and although Japan heaped concession upon concession, in the hope of finding a solution through mutual compromise, there was no progress because the United States would not retreat from its original position. Finally, in the end, the United States repeated demands that, under the circumstances, Japan could not accept: complete withdrawal of troops from China, repudiation of the Nanking government, withdrawal from the Tripartite Pact." [47]

---

[47] *The Journal for Historical Review*, Vol. 12, No. 1, Spring 1992, Hideki Tojo's Prison Diary, 41-42. The Tripartite Pact signed on 27 September 1940 was a ten year agreement between Germany, Italy and Japan. Its primary purpose was to maintain their new economic order based on usury free banking and to promote the mutual prosperity and welfare of their respective peoples. Article 3 provided for mutual

Numerous diplomatic initiatives were made by Japan, including the offer of a summit on 8 August 1941, but they all failed. By 2 December 1941 Japan had been cut off from 75% of her normal trade by the Allied blockade and thus found herself forced into attacking America in order to maintain her prosperity and to secure her existence as a sovereign nation. The uncompromising and unrelenting pressure applied by the usurers in New York had deliberately provoked Japan into taking retaliatory action.

Post World War II Developments

Following Japan's defeat one of the first acts of the United States occupation forces in Japan in September 1945 was to restructure the Japanese banking system, so as to make it compliant with the norms of the international bankers i.e. usury. The unrestricted financing of the state by the Bank of Japan was abolished and the large industrial combines, the *Zaibatsu*, were dismantled. This policy was carried out by Joseph Dodge, a Detroit banker, who was financial adviser to the Supreme Allied Commander, General Douglas MacArthur. The Ministry of Finance was, however, able to retain a measure of control over the banking system and in particular monetary policy. In 1988 Japan was adversely affected by its compliance with the Basel I regulations, which obliged the Bank of Japan to raise the minimum capital requirements of its risk-related assets from 2% to 8%. This action precipitated an on-off recession which has lasted for the past 29 years.

In April 1998 the Ministry of Finance was forced by law to yield to the independent Bank of Japan. Since that time the Bank of Japan has functioned as a typical Rothschild controlled central bank, which seldom performs its duties in the best interests of the Japanese people.

---

political, economic and military assistance, if one of the three powers was attacked by a power not then involved in the European war or Japanese-Chinese conflict.

Chapter VII

Modern Forms of State Banking

Banking was conceived in iniquity and was born in sin. The bankers own the earth. Take it away from them, but leave them the power to create deposits, and with a flick of the pen they will create enough deposits to buy it back again. However, take it away from them, and all the great fortunes like mine will disappear and they ought to disappear, for this would be a happier and better world to live in. But, if you wish to remain the slaves of the bankers and pay the cost of your own slavery, let them continue to create deposits."

– Sir Josiah Stamp former director of the Bank of England

Bank of North Dakota[1]

In 1919, the 48 states of the United States were offered the opportunity of setting up their own state banks. North Dakota was the only state which accepted this offer.

North Dakota, capital Bismarck, has a population of 790,000. It is situated in the middle of America on the Canadian border. Notwithstanding its harsh winters, its primary source of both direct and indirect income is agriculture. It ranks first in the United States in the production of wheat, mainly durum,[2] barley, canola, flaxseed, oats and sunflower seeds. Shale oil obtained by fracking in the Bakken basin and lignite are the state's principal mining products.

Most of the states of America are technically insolvent, and with the exception of North Dakota and her western neighbour

---

1   http://banknd.nd.gov/

2   A hard form of wheat used to make spaghetti and other kinds of pasta.

Montana, all have been experiencing budget deficits. By way of comparison California, the largest state in economic terms and currently the world's twelfth largest economy, had a deficit of just under $23 billion in April 2013 and pays out $10.4 billion in interest annually. In 2012 its bond debt amounted to $167.9 billion. In contrast to the other 49 states, which have been suffering rising levels of unemployment, North Dakota's unemployment rate has decreased and is currently the lowest in the USA at 2.7%. It also has the lowest default rates in the country.

In September 2012 North Dakota had a budget surplus of $1.6 billion. Between 1997 and 2010 its GDP grew by 93.4% from $16 billion to $31 billion. During the period 2000-11 personal income per capita increased by 127% from $20,155 to $45,747, while the national increase was 37.4% over the same period.

The secret of its success lies in its state bank. The mission statement of the bank is to provide sound financial services that promote agriculture, commerce and industry. By law the state must deposit all its funds in the bank, which pays a competitive rate of interest to the state treasurer.

The bank pays over all its profits to the state, which in 2011 were $60 million. Over $450 million has been paid to the state in the past 11 years. Most of these funds are used to offset taxes. The bank also provides a secondary market for real estate loans, guarantees for new business ventures and loans for farmers at an interest rate of 1% per annum. There has been no credit crisis or credit freeze in North Dakota, as the bank provides the state's own credit. By having established its own economic sovereignty, North Dakota has become the most financially viable and prosperous state in the USA.

In 2015 the North Dakota Legislative Assembly established a Bank of North Dakota Infrastructure Loan Fund programme which made $50 million in funds available to communities with a population of less than 2,000, and $100 million available to communities with a

North Dakota's thriving state bank which was founded by
a coalition of farmers in 1919.

population greater than 2,000. These loans have a 2% fixed interest rate of return and a term of up to 30 years. The proceeds can be used for the new construction of water and treatment plants, sewer and water lines, transportation infrastructure and other similar needs to support new growth in a community.

While state banking will not resolve the financial impasse being experienced at national level, state banks in the USA have the potential to provide considerable relief at state government level – budget surpluses, lower taxes, less unemployment and higher levels of prosperity. As at December 2016 there were 25 states considering some form of state banking legislation.[3]

The States of Guernsey

In 1815 after the Napoléonic wars had ended, Guernsey was in a precarious state. Its roads were in disrepair, the dykes were collapsing and the economy had slumped. The island was unable to borrow money as it could not raise the taxes to pay the required interest. In 1816 in order to fund public works and a new market place, the Committee of the States of Guernsey devised a novel

3   http://publicbankinginstitute.org/

The Old Market Place, St Peter Port, Guernsey was financed in 1816 by the issue of £6,000 in interest free and debt free bank notes.

solution. It issued £6,000 in one pound notes free of debt and interest. Within two years all the works had been completed without any addition to the state debt.[4]

A further £5,000, some of them in denominations of five pound notes, were authorised in 1824 to rebuild the Elizabeth College, founded by Queen Elizabeth I in 1563, and parochial schools. By 1837 £55,000 were in circulation. The island experienced increased trade and tourism and levels of prosperity not previously seen.

In 1914 The States notes issued had increased to £142,000. In 1937 the figure was £175,000. The cost of printing these notes was £450 compared to an annual interest charge of £11,383 per annum (6.5%). By 1958 there were £542,765 in existence. Currently there are £43.8 million in circulation.[5] Today

---

4   In their book The Guernsey Experiment, Distributionist Books, London, 1992, the Grubiaks provide the Grubiaks provide an interesting example of how compound interest can enslave a community. In 1817 the Glasgow Fruit Market was financed with an interest bearing loan of £60,000. It was eventually repaid 139 years later in 1956. The amount of interest expended between 1816 and 1910 is not known, but between 1910 and 1956 £267,886 was paid.

5   Treasury and Resources Department, Guernsey, 16 November 2012.

Guernsey has a population of 65,400 which enjoys one of the highest standards of living in the world. There is a flat income tax rate of 20% on world-wide income capped at £220,000 per annum. There is no company tax, except for a 10% tax on certain banking activities, no capital gains tax, no inheritance tax or estate duty, no purchase or sales tax, no value added tax (VAT) and no capital transfer tax. Guernsey has neither a national debt nor any external debt.

Central Bank of Libya

From 1551 to 1911 Libya was ruled by the Ottoman Empire, by Italy from 1911 to 1943 and from 1943 to 1951 was under the military suzerainty of Britain and France. The Central Bank of Libya was founded in 1956 and was run as a typical central bank until the bloodless *coup d'etat* of 1 September 1969.

Oil of an exceptionally high quality was discovered in 1959. However, King Idris al Mahdi as-Sanusi failed to capitalise on this bonanza or use it for the benefit of his people, and the bulk of the oil profits were siphoned into the coffers of the oil companies.

On assuming power in 1969 Mu'ammar Muhammad al-Qathafi took control of most of the economic activities in the country, including the central bank, which for all practical purposes was run as a state bank. It operated as a banker of the local bankers and foreign bankers were not permitted to operate. Financing of government infrastructure did not attract *riba* (interest) and Libya had no national debt and no foreign debt. Its foreign exchange reserves exceeded $54 billion, which may be compared to reserves of developed countries such as the United Kingdom and Canada, which in 2010 were $50 billion and $40 billion respectively. GDP growth during the period 2000-10 was 4.32% per annum and the official figure for inflation was -0.27%.[6]

---

6   www.theglobaleconomy.ca

Colonel[7] Qathafi was described by the mainstream media as being a "terrible dictator and a blood-sucking monster"[8], but the reality was that with the exception of the city of Benghazi and its environs, he had the support of 90% of the population.[9]

The following benefits provided by Qathafi explain why he was so popular.

- Free education.

- Students were paid the average salary for which subject they were studying.

- Students studying overseas were provided with accommodation, an automobile and €2,500 per annum.

- Free electricity.

- Free health care.

- Free housing (There were no mortgages).

- Newly-wed couples received a gift of 60,000 dinar ($50,000)[10] from government.

- Automobiles were sold at factory cost free of interest.

- Private loans were provided free of interest.

- Bread cost 15 US cents per loaf.

- Gasoline cost 12 US cents per litre.

- Portion of profits from sale of oil was paid directly into bank accounts of citizens.

- Farmers received free land, seeds and animals.

- Full employment with those temporarily unemployed paid a full salary as if employed.

---

7   His actual rank was that of a lieutenant.

8   http://embassy-finder.com/libya_in_kuwait_kuwait

9   Notwithstanding NATO's incessant bombing of Libya, on 1 July 2011 one million inhabitants of Tripoli (population 2.2. million) turned out in a rally in support of their brother leader Qathafi.

10   $1 = 1.20 Libyan dinar.

Mu'ammar Qathafi - A strict disciple of the Holy Q'uran, who abolished all forms of usury and used the Central Bank of Libya for the sole benefit of the Libyan people.

Qathafi's Jamahariya "state of the masses" ensured that the wealth of this country of 5.79 million inhabitants was fairly distributed to all of its people. Beggars and homeless vagrants did not exist, while life expectancy at 75 years was the highest in Africa and 10% above the world average. The literacy rate was 82%. Regarding human rights Libya stood at 61 in the International Incarceration Index. The lower the rating, the lower the standing. The no.1 spot is currently occupied by the United States.[11]

Another major achievement, which Qathafi initiated was the conversion of the Nubian Sandstone Fossil Aquifer System into the Great Man-Made River, which supplies 6,500,000m^3 of fresh water daily to the cities of Tripoli, Sirte and Benghazi. The extracted water is ten times cheaper than desalinated water. The total cost of the project, estimated at $25 billion was financed without a single foreign loan.

---

11   S. Goodson, *The Truth About Libya*, 4 April 2011, http://rense.com/general/93/truth. htm

Although the central banks of Belarus, Burma, Cuba, Iran, North Korea, North Sudan and Syria do not fall under the direct control of the Rothschild banking syndicate, Libya had the only central bank run on genuine state banking lines, which exhibited the classic symptoms of full employment, zero inflation and a modern day workers' paradise. The question arises as to why NATO intervened on the pretext of fabricated human rights abuses, the so called responsibility to protect. Since 1971 when the United States abandoned the gold exchange standard for the petrodollar with the connivance of Saudi Arabia, any attempt to displace the United States dollar as the premier reserve currency has been blocked and opposed with violence.

In November 2000 Saddam Hussein of Iraq decreed that all oil payments would in future be made in euros, as he did not wish to deal "in the currency of the enemy".[12] As has already been proven, the possession of weapons of mass destruction pretext was a deliberately concocted hoax and it was this currency decision, which cost Saddam Hussein his life and the destruction of his country. In similar circumstances Qathafi announced in 2010 the creation of the gold dinar as a replacement for the settlement of all foreign transactions in a proposed region of over 200 million people. Libya at that time possessed 144 tons of gold. What was intended was not a return to the gold standard *per se*, but a new unit of account with oil exports and other resources being paid for in gold dinars.[13] Qathafi crossed a red line and paid the ultimate price.

Since 2007 Iran has stipulated that payments be made in euro currency. On 17 February 2008 the Iranian Oil Bourse for trading in petroleum, petrochemicals and gas using primarily the euro, Iranian rial and a basket of non-US currencies was established. The first oil shipments under the new system were sold through this market in July 2011. This event must be deemed as one of the prime causes for the constant Israeli and American threats to annihilate Iran.

---

12   *Time*, 13 November 2000.

13   The Gold Dinar: Saving the World Economy from Gaddafi, www.globalresearch.ca ,
      5 May 2011.

Chapter VIII

The Banking Crisis

"I am afraid that the ordinary citizen will not like to be told that the banks can, and do, create and destroy money. The amount of money in existence varies only with the actions of the banks increasing and decreasing deposits and bank purchases...and they who control the credit of a nation, direct the policy of Governments and hold in the hollow of their hands the destiny of the people".[1]

– Reginald McKenna,
former Chancellor of the Exchequer.

Historical Overview

Banking crises generally take three forms, (i) where an individual bank collapses because of a lack of confidence and a subsequent withdrawal of deposits, (ii) a bank run when a number of banks fail simultaneously and (iii) when the entire system implodes.

In the eighteenth century banking crises were confined to only those countries which had central banks and practised usury viz. England, the Netherlands and Sweden.

In 1710 the Sword Blade Bank, in competition with the Bank of England, took over a portion of the National Debt in exchange for Sword Blade shares. The following year the South Sea Company did a similar deal and in 1720 took over the remaining government debt in exchange for its overvalued shares. The South Sea Company was nothing but a shell and had no trading assets. On 24 September 1720 the Sword Blade Bank went into liquidation and by the end of that year the shares of the South Sea Company had lost almost 90% of their peak value of £1,000 per share.

---

1   Chairman's address to shareholders of Midland Bank on 25 January 1924.

165

In 1763 after the end of the Seven Years War (1756-1763) *wissels* or bills issued by Dutch banker Leendert Pieter de Neufville could not be redeemed and precipitated a run on banks in the Netherlands, Germany and Sweden.

On 10 June 1772 the London banking house of Neal, James, Fordyce and Down, which had been indulging in speculation on a massive scale by shorting East India Company stock, crashed after it could no longer cover its losses by raiding customers' deposits. Twenty-two significant banks and almost all private banks in Scotland were forced into liquidation. The contagion then spread to Amsterdam. Many banks there experienced a liquidity crisis, including Clifford and Sons, which went bankrupt.

Henceforth almost all banking crises would be precipitated as a result of the central banking model which permits private banks to create money as an interest-bearing debt and then destroy it once it has been repaid. Thus the first two panics in the United States in 1792 and 1796-1797 were induced by the First Bank of the United States when it purposely withheld credit in order to cause a slump.

A similar financial disaster and subsequent depression were planned and executed by the Rothschild owned Second Bank of the United States in 1819, while England was also afflicted by artificially created panics in 1825 and 1847. In the panic of 1825 66 banks were forced to close their doors.

There was another banking panic in the United States in 1857 as a result of a fabricated shortage of gold and the failure of the Ohio Life Insurance and Trust Company. As has already been observed in Chapter IV, once the United States was forced on to the gold standard in January 1873, a pattern of more frequent and intensified banking panics evolved. Less than eight months later in September of that year the United States was premeditatedly plunged into a recession which lasted for four years.

The ensuing panics of 1884, 1890, 1890-1, 1893-4, 1897, 1903 and 1907 were all deliberately orchestrated so as to drive the American people into a state of confusion and despair. After 40 years of planned chaos, of boom and bust, as well as a targeted media campaign of disinformation, the population meekly capitulated and the banking conspirators' dream of a United States central bank was realised on 23 December 1913.

After the Great Depression which had been contrived by the US Federal Reserve Bank[2] a relative period of stability supervened until the 1990s when an ever increasing number of countries suffered economic crises and financial difficulties. (Finland, Sweden, Venezuela, Indonesia, South Korea, Thailand, Russia, Argentina, Ecuador and Uruguay).

The Banking Crisis 2007-

The seeds of the current banking crisis were sown when the Glass-Steagall Act of 1933, which prohibited bank holding companies from owning financial institutions and separated banks from investment houses, was abrogated on 12 November 1999. At the time of the promulgation of the original Act, Senator Carter Glass, a former US Secretary of the Treasury and one of its authors, remarked that "With a gun a man can rob a bank, with a bank a man can rob the world".

It was deemed towards the end of President Clinton's administration that everyone had the right to own a home, and for this purpose the Department of Housing and Development initiated a programme called National Homeownership Strategy Partners in the American Dream. In order to attract as many new homeowners as possible credit standards and regulations were relaxed and government allowed borrowers a tax credit of $8,000. Low teaser interest rates were offered

---

2   In 2002 in response to a question posed by Professor Milton Friedman to Ben Bernanke, then serving on the Academic Advisory Panel of the US Federal Reserve Bank of New York, about the Great Depression, Bernanke replied, "Regarding the Great Depression. You're right we did it. We're very sorry".

for the first two years, but with substantially higher rates being payable thereafter.

Between 1998 and 2006 house prices rose by 124%, but two years later in 2008, a drop of 20% was recorded. In contrast to rising prices, the affordability of housing showed a declining trend. Between 1980-2000 the ratio of the cost of an average house to median household income was 3.0, but by 2006 it had risen to 4.6. Credit default swaps which were intended to hedge or speculate against credit risks increased hundredfold between 1998 and 2008 to $47 trillion and had a notional value of $683 trillion.

In order to fuel the property boom, innovative financial products were developed such as collaterised debt obligations. Mortgages of varying degrees of quality were bundled up and after having been assessed, fraudulently as it transpired, by rating agencies as being triple A in many cases, were sold on to gullible investors.[3] In order to further this culture of greed the shadow banking sector which includes investment banks and hedge funds and whose total funds were believed at that time to have amounted to in excess of $100 trillion, aggressively marketed these products, notwithstanding the fact that by June 2007 39% of all home loans did not meet the underwriting standards of any issuer.

The balloon finally went up when Lehmann Brothers was declared bankrupt on 15 September 2008. A rescue package was hastily assembled and Congress approved a sum of $700 million for a Troubled Asset Relief Program (TARP), but this was only the tip of the iceberg, as the US Federal Reserve Bank has since granted over $16 trillion worth of assistance to domestic and foreign banks. According to the memoir[4] of Neil Barofsky,

3   One of the more spectacular victims of this fraud was the Oil Fund of The Government Pension Fund of Norway, the second largest sovereign wealth fund in the world, which recorded a loss of $90 billion in 2008. This loss effectively wiped out all the profits of the previous 12 years. http://news.bbc.co.uk/2/hi/business/7961100.stm

4   N. Barofsky, *Bailout: An Inside Account of How Washington Abandoned Main Street While Rescuing Wall Street*, Free Press, New York, 2012, 288 pp. In November 2011 The Levy Economics Institute, Bard College, New York calculated that the total bailout added up to $29 trillion.

Inspector General of the TARP, the final figure may well exceed $24 trillion. It therefore comes as no surprise that during the period 2008-2013 the US Federal Reserve Bank has expanded its balance sheet by 500% to $5 trillion in order to prop up an insolvent banking sector with its Ponzi-like[5] quantitative easing programme, while in similar vein between 2007 and 2012 the balance sheets of the six largest western banks have been inflated by 36.4% from $10.7 trillion to $14.6 trillion.

Causatum

In the aftermath of this financial crisis attempts have been made to remedy what is in essence an insoluble problem. The Dodd-Frank Wall Street Reform and Consumer Protection Act passed into law on 21 July 2010 contains numerous regulations designed to promote accountability, financial stability and transparency. 200 pages of the Act are devoted to mortgage reform and include higher underwriting standards and an obligation on mortgage originators to ensure that borrowers have the ability to repay their loans.

The sciolists of the Basel Committee on Banking Supervision have proposed higher levels of capital and liquidity ratios in the hope that these measures will strengthen the banking sector. The intention is that they be implemented in full by 31 March 2019. Regrettably, they will in all probability have the opposite outcome and will only cause the money supply to shrink further and thereby deepen the recession.

What is not understood by most bankers and economists is that the only method available for keeping the economy running is to sink further into debt (at interest), as debt based money is the only source of our means of exchange. Hence the persistent mantra that growth must be maintained at all costs, because if all loans were to be repaid, the money supply would vanish, and we

---

5   Charles Ponzi an American con artist and swindler of the early twentieth
     century.

would be reduced to exchanging goods and services with bank notes and barter. In the current situation a world-wide debt cancellation would therefore not be out of place, if the money supply could be replaced by state bank created interest free and debt free money.

The underlying reason why the developed world, which has in the past produced superior, long-lasting products, has been partially deindustrialised, is so that inferior goods have to be continually produced by third world countries in order to fuel the growth syndrome. It also highlights the absurdity of the insistence that Europe needs economic growth when its indigenous population is shrinking. This policy of deliberately planned obsolescence and forced growth also has very deleterious effects on the environment. As will be observed in the final section, the collapse in female fertility rates in the developed world, which is a direct consequence of usury, will lead to the extinction of civilisation.

In conclusion it may be stated that the principal hidden purpose of the banking crisis is to create a general feeling of desperation and an acclamation for a solution such as a World Central Bank - a similar situation which prevailed in the United States during the late nineteenth century when banking panics were being artificially created in preparation for the imposition of the US Federal Reserve Bank. Whether the parasitic bankers will achieve this objective is open to doubt as the host may well have vanished by then.

The Great Depression of the 21st Century

One of the primary causes of the ballooning debt bubble has been the suicidal policy of globalisation and free trade, which has resulted in the afore-mentioned partial deindustrialisation of the United States, United Kingdom and Europe. The relocation of industries to third world countries has precipitated a reduction in the manufacturing base of the developed world, structural unemployment of a permanent nature and a widening trade gap. In an attempt to maintain their falling standards of living, consumers in these affected countries have been forced to take on increasing levels of personal debt. Thus in the United States during the 1980s $2.37 of private debt were required to produce $1 of growth in GDP, in the 1990s the figure rose to $2.99, and in the 2000s there was a dramatic increase to $5.67 for each incremental dollar of economic growth – a level which will soon become untenable.

A further aggravating factor is that the rising cost of extracting energy, also known as the energy returns on energy invested (EROEI) is rapidly approaching a tipping point. According to a Tullett Prebon report,[6] in 1990 the theoretical cost of energy would have been 2.43% of GDP[7] and in 2010 it almost doubled to 4.7% of GDP. It is predicted to rise to 9.6% of GDP by 2020 and to 15% by 2030. This decline in energy returns, which will cause the wide spread closure of mines and industries, and adversely affect agriculture, predicates a very substantial drop in living standards.[8]

Escalating extraction costs of energy are not the only predicament facing mankind. During the past 100 years water consumption has quadrupled and continues to rise. Currently 1.6 billion people are facing absolute water scarcity and according to a recent US government report in June 2014, global demand for water will exceed supply by 40% by 2030.[9]

---

6   T.M. Morgan, *Perfect storm energy, finance and end of growth* www.tullettprebon.com/ Documents/strategyinsights/TPSI009PerfectStorm009.pdf

7   Professor Frederick Soddy's so called flamboyant period before entropy ensues, which in this case means the depletion of relatively scarce terrestrial materials.

8   Virtually all agricultural land was under cultivation by 1960. Between 1950 and 1984, for example, global grain production increased by 280%. However, the increases in agricultural production have been almost entirely dependent on energy inputs used in planting (fertilizers), harvesting, processing and distribution. Sustained increases in energy inputs could reduce food production by almost half.

9   http://theeconomiccollapseblog.com/archives/25-shocking-facts-about-theearths-dwindling-water-resources

However, the factor which overrides all these macro economic considerations is the collapse in the birth rate of the developed world. At the turn of the twentieth century the White population of the world numbered 590 million or 36% of its 1.65 billion total. In 2016 although that number had increased absolutely to 1 billion, its relative share of the world's population of 7.5 billion has shrunk to 13.3%. Two fratricidal and pointless world wars over the maintenance of the usury system set this catastrophic decline in motion.

The following table of fertility rates[10] reveals the inevitability and the near mathematical certainty that by 2100 most of the Whites and a large portion of the Asian peoples of north east Asia will have died out.

Nigeria	5.32
Pakistan	3.52
Egypt	2.89
Bangladesh	2.83
India	2.81
Indonesia	2.18
Mexico	2.21

The first column of the table of fertility rates above lists all countries with a population in excess of 100 million, while the following table lists the populations of the major White and Far East Asian countries.

The accepted fertility rate for the replacement of a population is 2.11.[11] Thus the White, Chinese and Japanese populations will be severely depleted within three generations,[12] and unless the

10 www.en.wikipedia.org/wiki/List-of-sovereign-states-and-dependent-territories-by-fertility-rate
11 The average fertility rate of the world is 2.55, but it is not clear whether this figure has been calculated arithmetically or is a weighted average.
12 With the average age of a woman in the developed world giving birth to her first child having risen to 30 years, a generation now lasts 30 as opposed to the previous average of 25 years 40 years ago

fertility rate substantially increases will face eventual extinction.

USA	2.05
U.K.	1.94
Brazil	1.90
France	1.89
Australia	1.79
Sweden	1.67
Canada	1.53
Germany	1.41
Spain	1.41
Italy	1.38
Russia	1.34
Japan	1.27
China	1.05
South Africa	2.64 The white fertility rate is 1.5

From the above table it may be noted that a fertility rate of 1.3 would take 80-100 years to reverse, which is well nigh impossible; while historically a fertility rate of 1.9 has never been reversed. Moreover the sharpness of the decline in the White population is concealed by virtue of the fact that large numbers of non-Whites, who have much higher rates of fertility, are included in these fertility rates.

The percentage of whites in the following major countries is as follows:

Brazil	48
Germany	88 [13]
United Kingdom	86 [14]
Australia	85

---

13   According to the German statistics office Destatis, 15 million or 19% of Germany's population of 80.2 million were of a non-German background. The census was conducted on 9 May 2011. Since 2015 an estimated 1.5 million non-European immigrants have entered Germany.

14   *Heritage and Destiny*, The Changing Face of a Disunited Kingdom, Preston, England, March-April 2013, 3.

France	85
Russia	81
Canada	80
United States	65 [15]

Much reliance has been placed on China, which it is hoped will save the world economy from its demise, but the fertility rates of neighbouring territories of Hong Kong (population 7 million) of 0.97 and Taiwan (population 23.3 million) of 1.10 are indicative of a declining trend, and are matched by mainland China's fertility rate of 1.05. These declining fertility rates in China are also underpinned by the one child policy of the Chinese government, which has been in effect since 1979. It is anticipated that China will achieve zero population growth in the near future.

Since World War II ever increasing numbers of married women in the Western world, deluded by the malevolent propaganda of feminism and gender equality, have been forced to seek employment, so that their families can pay the ever increasing amounts of interest necessary in order to make ends meet. Most of this interest is accrued on mortgage loans i.e. on money which banks have created out of nothing. The direct result of this iniquitous financial system has been the undermining of normal family life and a dramatic reduction in female fertility. According to Aaron Russo the Rockefellers were behind this diabolical scheme which was created to draw women into the income tax net, place their children in school at an early age where they could be indoctrinated, destabilise society and set up the New World Order[16]. In this manner the link between usury and demographic decline has been established. Even if the usury system should be abolished in its entirety within the next five to ten years, these trends will not be easily reversed over both the short and medium term. If usury remains intact, then the world must brace itself for a depression, similar to the Dark Ages, which will last for many centuries.

15   M. Merlin, *Our Vision for America*, A2Z Publications LLC, Las Vegas, 2012, ix.

16   See https://www.youtube.com/watch?v=zCpjmvaIgNA where the late Mr. Aaron Russo, a friend of Council on Foreign Relations member Nicholas Rockefeller, also reveals that Gloria Steinem's *Ms. Magazine* was financed by the CIA.

In the preceding chapters it has been proven, conclusively, that state banking and the sovereign issue of a nation's money supply are the only means for the provision of a natural order of harmony, peace and prosperity founded on the ethnic independence of all peoples.

The past 300 years, notwithstanding numerous technological advancements, have witnessed a progressive deterioration in Western and European standards of civilisation. The excessive concentration of power and wealth, based exclusively on dishonest banking methods, has enabled a tiny minority of criminal bankers to control the media and educational processes, and thereby to brainwash a mindless and atomised humanity, deluded by the spurious comforts of democracy and materialism, into suicidal practices of savage, bloody and pointless wars, central banking and cultural degradation, which will eventually result in its demographic extinction.

Thank you for the exceptionally interesting article[1] you just sent me, as well as for the book you sent me in October, that my wife and I have read with great interest. –

Prince Dimitri Romanovich Romanov

Rungsted
Denmark

September 2015.

Appendix I

Letter from President Abraham Lincoln

Chicago
Illinois
December 1864

Colonel E D Taylor
I have long determined to make public the origin of the greenback and tell the world that it is one of Dick Taylor's creations. You have always been friendly to me, and when troublous times fell upon us, and my shoulders, though broad and willing, were weak and myself surrounded by such circumstances and such people that I knew not whom to trust, then I said in my extremity, "I will send for Colonel Taylor; he will know what to do." I think it was in January 1862, on or about the 16th, that I did so. You came, and I said to you, "What shall we do?" Said you, "Why, issue treasury notes bearing no interest, printed on the best banking paper. Issue enough to pay off the army expenses, and declare it legal tender." Chase thought it a hazardous thing, but we finally accomplished it, and gave to the people of this Republic the greatest blessing they ever had – their own paper to pay off their own debts. It is due to you, the father of the present greenback that the people should know it, and I take great pleasure in making it known. How many times I have laughed at you telling me plainly that I was too lazy to be anything but a lawyer.

Yours truly

A Lincoln

The text above is from a hand written letter by President Abraham Lincoln, which was verified and documented on 10 February 1888 by the 50th United States Congress.

Appendix II

The Social Crediter, Saturday, May 6th, 1939.

THE SOCIAL CREDITER
FOR POLITICAL AND ECONOMIC REALISM

Vol. 2, No. 8.   Registered at G.P.O. as a Newspaper.   SATURDAY, MAY 6th, 1939.   3d. Weekly.
Postage (home and abroad) 1d.

LETTER TO HERR HITLER

Publication of the following letter, addressed to the Fuehrer and despatched through a trustworthy channel, is authorised by Major Douglas.

May, 1939.

Herr Fuehrer,

As an introduction to the attached memorandum,* I would request permission to bring to the notice of your eminent self the following observations:—

(a) While it is claimed, and is no doubt sincerely believed, that there is some conflict of ideologies between the 'democratic' group of Powers and the Totalitarian group, there is, in fact, no such conflict—all of them proceed equally from the fundamental assumption, which is no doubt believed to be indisputable, that full employment of their populations is the test of success.   Their differences are of method only.

(b) If this claim rests on a 'moral' basis, then it must be observed that it raises up practical problems which appear to be only soluble by recourse to a war of mutual destruction certain to result in anarchy and final subjection to a Transatlantic survivor.

(c) If, however, it is claimed that full employment is a practical requirement of an advancing civilisation, it can easily be shown that the contrary is the case.   While it is recognised that the present production of armaments in every country has been forced by the general assumption that unemployment is equivalent to economic destruction, it must yet be obvious that the full employment which armaments provide is both temporary and at the same time perhaps the ultimate example of waste and inefficiency.

(d) This employment policy, which is here challenged, is now recognised to be inseparable from the Jewish Financial System.

(e) A simple change in this system would make full employment unnecessary, eliminate the competition for markets and destroy the power of the international Financier—a power which war only increases and which, if not destroyed, will destroy civilisation in Europe.

May I earnestly request that the present crisis may, in the key position in the history of the world, which you hold, be used to force an exposure of this false and destructive policy?

It is indisputable that, if this were to be made the major issue of any such conference as has been proposed, not only Germany but the whole civilised world would be united in support of the action taken by you.   Not President Roosevelt, but yourself, would be recognised as the representative of all those values which are cherished equally in the so-called democracies and their artificially created antagonists.

Yours truly,

C.H. Douglas

Letter from C.H. Douglas to Adolf Hitler in May 1939 urging Hitler to oppose the "Jewish Financial System" as a "representative of all those values which are cherished equally in the so-called democracies and their artificially created antagonists"

178

Appendix III

Federal Reserve Note - Plutocratic money issued by the privately owned US Federal Reserve Bank.

Genuine government-issued money in circulation from 1862-1994.

On 4 June 1963 President John F. Kennedy issued Executive Order No. 11110 which instructed the Treasury to print $4 billion worth of $2 and $5 bills. These bills, backed by silver in the Treasury's vaults, were issued free of debt and interest with the seigniorage accruing not to the privately owned US Federal Reserve Bank, but to the US government. This note issue formed part of Kennedy's long term plan to reduce the power of the US Federal Reserve Bank. On 22 November 1963 Kennedy was shot down by assassin(s) in Dallas, Texas.

Review by Matthew Johnson

One of the most difficult things to explain to American university students is how capitalism and communism share far more in common than they do in conflict. In fact, regardless of how it is explained, the old saw that the two approaches are "opposites" can never quite penetrate. Even worse, explaining to students and their bewildered parents that the US banking and industrial conglomerates financed the Soviet Red revolution and built Soviet industry is also maddeningly impossible.

One simple way to explain it is to say that, for bankers in the modern era, the state's control of the entire economy from one place is what bankers believe paradise to look like. There is one plan, one banking system and one social system in place; this means that banks merely forward the cash, both expecting the state, not the economy as such, to reimburse them with the requisite interest. In other words, the command economy is the most congenial to banks. There is no necessary connection between private banking and a state-owned economy. It is just as simple for a banker to work for the Party as it is for Goldman-Sachs.

Capitalism and socialism are based on materialism. Production and utility alone are considered goods, and efficiency in methods is considered the *sine qua non* of ethical contemplation. Both systems are oriented to technology, hold to a linear view of history, and seek the mechanization of all aspects of humanity. As they both develop, the economic system and the state merge into a single machine. The error of the libertarians has always been their insistence that the state and private capital are opposed. Quite the opposite is true. Large concentrations of capital are deeply embedded in the state, using it as both a personal bodyguard and as a regulator that keeps market entry impossibly high. The defeat of the Justice Department by Microsoft in 2010-2012 shows the imbalance of power between private capital and the state. This might seem tangential to a work on banking. For the typical isolated and tenured professor of political economy, it would be. For those, such as Mr. Goodson, who served on the Board of the Central Bank of South Africa for many years, isolated academia seems absurd. Mr. Goodson was anything but isolated, and he witnessed the tight control of economic life by banking conglomerates the world over. He saw it in vivid colors.

This book is not a study in technical economics. It is, thankfully, a study in history. Goodson realizes what most economists do not: that to grasp any economic phenomenon, it must be seen as a product of many decades of historical development. Each aspect of the whole continually reinforces the other, and the whole itself is constantly changing, like an organism, as history continues to present new challenges, new projects and new victims.

In other words, the secret life of banks did not merely occur because a group of men off the coast of Georgia wanted it to. They themselves were actors within a historical stream that goes back to the first Mesopotamian civilisations and reached its ancient zenith in Rome. The fact that the whole has continuously been based on the same set of assumptions regardless of the civilisation within which it was embedded is impressive, and it calls out for detailed analysis. Given the political fallout from such honesty, however, Mr. Goodson needed to resign himself to the fact that few in the mainstream will even mention his work, let alone accept it.

There is one constant in history that is manifestly clear in this work: that the essential distinction between monarchy and republicanism (broadly speaking) is economic. Republics are normally oligarchies, or at least contain its seeds. Monarchies, since they are perpetually at war with their own nobility, often reject the assumptions of oligarchy. Whether it be the national socialist party of China or Belarus, the royal bank of St. Petersburg or the centralised dictatorship of the Augustan era, all forms of strong statism have made war on the banking monopoly. No authoritarian leader will accept competition from an all powerful economic mediator. Of course, there are a few exceptions on both sides, but history has been fairly clear that strong states, those based on traditional authority, reject the alchemy of money and interest.

Rome

Rome rapidly, at the time of Cicero, was already moving away from its Senatorial oligarchy and towards the military empire of Sulla and his successors. The immediate impact, once the dust of the civil wars cleared, was that minting was centralised and usury controlled. Julius Caesar sought to limit interest to 1% monthly and, in a populist move rarely seen, banned its compound increase. Furthermore, any accumulated interest could never exceed the original principal.

In Byzantium, the Roman empire of the East, interest had been officially limited to 5%, give or take, but this could only be enforced under emperors who were strong. Basil II for example, rejected interest altogether and forced wealthy landowners to financially assist poorer peasants. His strength, while common, was usually followed by an aristocratic reaction who placed puppet emperors in Constantinople. However, under such a system, eastern Rome was blessed with a vibrant, populist economy. Her currency was the global standard as far east as China. Peasants were free landholders and feudalism existed nowhere. Inflation did not exist, and trade flows always favored the capital. For this reason, oligarchic states such as Venice, Dubrovnik and the Norman interlopers in Sicily, continually financed Rome's enemies.

After 1204, when the western Norman Crusaders sacked Constantinople, the dominance of Venetian oligarchs became the order of the day. Byzantium was marked for death once the emperors of the 14th and 15th century gave away their financial autonomy for regular infusions of Venetian money. Having lost all economic independence and seeing the immense wealth of the east flow in interest payments to Italy, Byzantium finally collapsed under an Italian-financed Turkish invasion in 1453. Venice became Turkey's most significant ally.

There is no economic mystery here. Whenever interest is tightly controlled, the continued compound leakage of cash to banking centers does not exist. This financial hemorrhaging means that value remains where it belongs: with the small businessman and small landholder. Without the geometrically increasing mass of interest, a fraction of today's total labor was sufficient to maintain monetary stability, necessary supplies and a nobility forced to serve the state rather than rule it. Within the modern system of usury, centralization is unavoidable as compound interest continually increases the flow of real value out of the economy and into the coffers of the cabal.

England

England was no different. Prior to the Norman invasion, Anglo-Saxon England, even after the Viking attacks, existed in a financial golden age. Again, smallholders were the norm, urban trade maintained low prices, and the lack of liquid capital forestalled any noble centralization. Feudalism could not exist under such a system. Usury was banned in Mercia under Offa the Great, and in Alfred's frantic attempt to centralize power in Wessex against the Danes, he too, refused the "services" of the banking cabal. The Italian banks, however, were quite interested in William's planned assault on Anglo-Saxondom and to remove Scandinavian influence from England. Following William was a small army of Jewish slave traders and Venetian and Roman bankers. Usury was permitted, for a time, under the new Norman hegemony. The old Anglo aristocracy was slaughtered, and William imported a new nobility with close ties to Italy. Feudalism made its very first appearance on English soil. Ireland, several centuries later, was also to see the benefits of Norman progress.

Such progress, by the time of Stephen, led to the creation of a banking system charging an average of 33% on collateral lands and 300% on capital (that is, tools in the cities). Within two generations, a full 66% of England's lands wound up in the hands of Italian and Jewish bankers. This might explain the constant drive to take more and more French land for the Angevin Empire.

This was to be the lot of Norman Britain until the reign of Edward I (d.1307), who imitated the Byzantines (where many Anglo-Saxons had been serving after 1066) by tightly limiting interest and its accumulation. Kicking the bankers out of the country, he ushered in an age of prosperity unfortunately cut short by the plague. It is no accident that just at the time when Byzantium had given away its economic sovereignty to Venice for the use of their navy, Britain moved in the opposite direction against Italy and Rome.

From the reign of Edward I to the plague, England was prosperous. The working year amounted to 14 weeks, within which all essentials were obtained. The church calendar, in both eastern and western Europe, required between 100 and 140 days off a year, excluding Sunday and the period after Easter. Of course, capitalism was to make war on the church and seek Protestant sanction for eliminating saints days from the calendar altogether. The rule of the small holder had returned for the first time since Edward the Confessor. Unfortunately, this was not to last. The reformation, once Luther's influence had waned, had different ideas on money.

Once Henry VII had stabilized Britain after the War of the Roses, the time was ripe for the rise of the banks yet again. The reformation and the immorality of Henry VIII gave it the excuse it needed. The reformation was an attempt by the Stuarts to begin centralizing power once the old nobility had slaughtered itself into oblivion. Monastic lands were secularized, land markets developed, and financing long distance trade became a priority. Henry VII became the last gasp of a powerful, traditional state. From Henry VIII to Edward VI to Elizabeth, a new oligarchy had gained power that required the pomp of monarchy to hide behind. Very soon, once it became confident in its role, it required William of Orange to justify itself.

Spain, once Islam was finally ejected, sought to cleanse itself of the Sephardi, normally allies of the Muslim Caliphate. Spain's nationalism was substantial as both church and state were radically reformed and purged. Moving to Amsterdam, the Sephardi rebuilt its banking base, creating a "square" of influence that contained four corners: the grain trade in the Baltic, the Amsterdam banks, Constantinople and the Turkish market, and most importantly, Poland. These represented the overland routes of modernity as grain prices skyrocketed in the west, forcing the east to export more and more.

Under Elizabeth and certainly during and after the English Revolution, Spain was the enemy. Catholic Ireland sought Spanish assistance against Elizabeth's dispossession of the native Gaels, something that Cromwell was to punish with genocidal harshness. Spain's importation of silver from the new world threatened the rule of the banks in a graphic way. The banking regime financed the Dutch rebellion against the Spanish as the world's press spared no rhetorical excess denouncing the Spanish army in northern Europe. British enemies of the banking elite looked to Spain for assistance as well.

Once Charles I was defeated in 1645 and Cromwell instituted a military dictatorship over Britain and Ireland in 1653, the banking regime now had its enemies destroyed and its place assured. William's gentle occupation of Winchester 30 years later meant that the bankers now had England to use against both France and Spain. It surprised no one that the Jacobites spent much time attacking the banking elite that had taken power with such vehemence. Neither James I or II believed in "divine right" nor did either want to impose a dictatorship. Cromwell alone sought that honor. Yet the James's were accused of every imaginable crime. James sought religious tolerance, not a "Spanish theocracy" as the Whigs were later to claim. Whiggery was the party of usury and, as such, the party most vehement in seeking war with France, Spain and, eventually, Russia.

Parliament, now the instrument of capitalism and empire, was seeking any excuse to take revenge on Spain. "Democracy" and "the will of the people" were considered identical to the interest of urban merchants and traders. Britain was now an oligarchy. Roman Catholic rulers were long forbidden to rule in London, regardless of James' desire for religious neutrality. William's war with France was financed by the Amsterdam banking establishment, something made quite clear to William himself when he tried to arrange a Stuart marriage, one which remained childless.

Ukraine and Poland

It is certainly no coincidence that the rule of Cromwell and the slow genocide of Irish resistors and English Jacobites occurred at the same time the opposite development was taking place on the other "pole" of the Jewish "trade square." Population growth in the west, as well as the growing centralization of states, led to an increase in grain demand. This meant, among other things, that the nobility needed to intensify its serfdom over peasants and force more production towards export.

The Polish nobility had given Jews a full monopoly over overland trade, urban life, lease-holding and alcohol. Mainstream sources on Ukrainian history all are forced to admit this. The impotent Polish monarchy sought to gain power, as the case elsewhere, through an alliance with the towns. Seeing this as a threat, the Polish nobles countered this by bringing in Khazar Jews searching for a new home after the fall of Italy centuries before. Not only did they find it, but their mainstream power and success reached such heights that rabbinic claims that the 17th century was a "messianic" time were common. In fact, it was a drumbeat that the time of the savior was at hand. They got the revolt of Cossack Hetman Bogdan Khmelnytsky instead. Khmelnytsky's revolt was the opposite of Cromwell's. The Cossacks fought against a long standing oligarchy, while Cromwell sought to establish one.

The rising of Khmelnytsky in 1648 was the single event that defined Ukrainian nationalism for eternity. Nothing was the same. Poland almost collapsed. Jews had to flee for their lives. The Crimean Tartars were able to free themselves from vassalage to Turkey. Rome was in a panic as their churches, long associated with usury, were burnt to the ground by Cossacks, well remembering that their existence was based on the ruins of Orthodox churches a century before. Still reeling from the Reformation, Rome now faced the eradication of its existence in the east too. The Patriarch of Jerusalem, Paisios, declared Hetman Khmelnytsky "The Monarch of All Rus." Russia, Vienna, Prussia and Paris were now able to centralize power and defy Rome. Russia had a particular gripe with Rome since it was the papacy who declared a Crusade against northern Russia in 1256, financed Mongol expansion, and declared the Polish attack on Ukraine a "holy war." While Paris and Vienna remained Catholic, theirs was a national Catholicism where the crown, not Rome, began selecting bishops. It was not to last.

Rome managed to talk the Crimeans into abandoning the Orthodox Slavs. The death of Hetman Khmelnytsky in 1657 led to a division in the Cossack host between hetmans of the two banks of the Dnieper at war with each other. Hetman Ivan Vyhovsky and Pavlo Teteria sought a Polish alliance, Briukhovetsky in the east went to Moscow, and Doroshenko, in desperation, went to the Turks. In 1708, Hetman Ivan Mazepa went to the Swedes. Disaster resulted and, among Ukrainian historians, this period was known as the "Ruin."

As Russia moved closer to the Dnieper, Vienna became alarmed at the possible Russification of most of the east (including the Balkans) and mobilized against her. Given some breathing room, Poland recovered her former stability and the nobles returned. A century later, the Cossack Haidaimak rebellions led to the unthinkable: the treaty of "eternal friendship" (that is, the Treaty of Andrusovo, 1667) between Poland and Russia dividing Ukraine between the two empires. The Haidaimak rebellion was crushed by a concerted effort of Moscow and Krakow, and all was precisely as it was before 1648.

Like in England, under Cossack rule, society was divided into counties, with full local democracy and a total lack of interest and usury. The typical results followed: the traditional Slavic smallholder communities reemerged and a basic political and economic equality resulted. The slow encouragement of a Cossack aristocracy, financed by St. Petersburg, led to the imposition of an oligarchy that made it very easy for Catherine II in the middle 18th century to put an end to the Hetmanate forever.

The United States

The decentralised colonies of the US were generally prosperous. Plentiful land, excellent ports and a strong pioneer spirit created an advanced world out of practically nothing. When asked about this, Benjamin Franklin famously remarked:

That is simple. In the colonies we issue our own money. It is called colonial script. We issue it in the proper proportion to the demands of trade and industry to make the products pass easily from the producers to the consumers. In this manner, creating for ourselves our own paper money, we control its purchasing power, and we have no interest to pay anyone. (Benjamin Franklin in London, 1763, quoted from Goodson, 66).

With one exception – the execrable Alexander Hamilton – the

American founders, though differing on nearly every other issue, were of one mind on banking. It was something to be abhorred. The dollar remained stable until 1917. The boom and bust cycles since the Civil War, the immense rise in federal power, World War I and the coming American empire, however, helped set the stage for a privately owned cabal in the US as well, popularly known as the "Fed" or the Federal Reserve ("Federal" in this case should be taken as it is in the shipping company "Federal Express").

The fact is that the fears of the Anti-Federalists were correct: the US government in Washington had become extremely powerful, arrogant and cut off from the common run of Americans. They had long been in thrall to the oligarchy in embryo, soon to burst forth in the form of the Fed, the Rockefeller Empire, the Carnegie Cult, and the warfare state tested in the Spanish American war and in the final months of World War I.

From 1914 to 1920, prices rose 125%, as Goodson depressingly recounts. The dollar lost almost 60% of its value in six years. Federal bonds saw their value drop by 20% at the same time, meaning that older bonds became more expensive. Yet, the newer, cheaper bonds led to a recall by the banks which, of course, means that the money came due.

More instability was caused as the railroads and other modes of transport prices went through the roof. Small farms, the long standing backbone of American prosperity, were slowly priced out of existence, which, in practice, meant a massive wealth transfer from the countryside to the cities. Agricultural production dropped by 50%. The war on rural America was declared, and has yet to end. The deficit was soon to be made up by Agribusiness, made possible by centralised credit that sought to finance large conglomerates, seen as a safer bet, rather than small businesses.

In 1927, the Fed lowered rates and thus, increased the money supply. But this was the reign of the "roaring twenties," the beginning of the oligarchy as an exposed, confident entity without serious opposition. This meant that money was seen as value and power in its own right, separate from actual production. The money went to the stock market, boosting demand and inflating prices. Margins were increased through debt, and the price-earnings ratio went as high as 50:1, that is to say, the stock price was many times higher than the actual productive nature of the capital involved. Put differently, stock prices had no relation to the health of the firms involved, the productivity of capital or labor, or the resultant value added.

Thus, in 1927, the US stock market was a fraud. Prices were based on speculative investment, easy money and the perception, one that remains a mystery to psychiatry, that such faux-growth would last forever. It made little difference how healthy the firms involved actually were. In 1929, the Fed increased rates to 6%. The signal was clear: the stock market, as a whole, saw its value drop by 83%. 10,000 banks were bankrupted, and brokers, working on debt bubbles, were ruined.

Russia

Russian economic prosperity and growth commenced at the liberation of the serfs by Alexander II in 1861. Serfs under state control had been freed earlier by Tsar Nicholas I. As is quite often the case, the most autocratic of monarchs were the only ones confident enough to go over the heads of the elites and pass legislation in the interests of the peasants. Unlike the Austrian liberation of its own serfs a few years before and Lincoln's freeing of southern slaves, Russian serfs were liberated with land. The state reimbursed the eternally indebted nobility and, over time, the peasant was to pay the state back. The payments were very low and Tsar Nicholas II in 1905 canceled them altogether. This was just one more nail in the nobility's coffin.

Russian serfs had never been slaves. Serfdom, a reaction to the Swedish and Polish invasions of the 17th century, affected only peasants in the black earth regions in the Russian south. It never existed in the north nor in Siberia. In central Russia, it affected only serfs required to perform labor dues, but by the 1840s, most peasants paid money rent, meaning that they were not serfs. Serfdom, in Russia, really meant the guarantee of peasant land ownership and, at the same time, the guarantee of noble incomes as they served the state, usually in a military capacity. Since everyone served someone, the system was balanced. Under Tsar Paul and his mother Catherine II, the nobles were freed from state service and, as a result, became politically impotent.

Peasants had full self government in the commune, where all posts were elected. The *volost*, or county, government was also entirely elected, with equal representation for all classes. The court system both at the *volost* and commune level, too, was based on pure peasant democracy. Commune judges were exclusively peasants, and *volost* courts had two noble and two peasant representatives. For the most part, Russian nobles were financially worse off than the peasantry, drowning in debt and long released from state service. They had little to do but buy expensive western luxuries they could not afford. The peasant commune had the right to nullify federal law, and was generally self-sufficient. If anything, tsarist Russia suffered from too much democracy.

In 1861, the *volost* was replaced by the *zemstvo*, a strong county system with a lower house of peasants and an upper house of nobles, usually poor. The *zemstvo* was in charge of education, infrastructure, church life, tax collection and police. There was no part of peasant life that was not based on local democracy. A "land captain," usually a poor noble, was elected to mediate disputes between peasants and nobles, and sometimes, peasants would go to the captain if he had a beef with the commune or the *zemstvo* authorities. Politically speaking, from 1850 on, the nobles were politically impotent.

Hence, the freedom of the serfs and the creation of a free press, the *zemstvo* and an endless array of educational reforms put a bullet in the revolutionary movement, almost entirely financed from Britain. Seeing this as intolerable, Alexander II was assassinated for his trouble in 1881. His son, Alexander III, continued his father's reform programs but, being a man of immense size and toughness, smashed the revolutionary movement, making it toothless until his untimely death in 1894.

Tsar Alexander III established the Peasant Land Bank in the early 1880s, which gave interest-free loans to peasants and sought to channel investment money into agricultural improvement. Tsar Alexander and his finance minister, Nikolai Bunge, drafted and passed the most comprehensive labor regulations in European history. His son, Nicholas II, continually added to them until the outbreak of World War I.

In labour relations the Russians were pioneers. Child labour was abolished over 100 years before it was abolished in Great Britain in 1867. Russia was the first industrialised country to pass laws limiting the hours of work in factories and mines. Strikes, which were forbidden in the Soviet Union, were permitted and minimal in Tsarist times. Trade union rights were recognized in 1906, while an Inspectorate of Labour strictly controlled working conditions in factories. In 1912 social insurance was introduced. Labour laws were so advanced and humane that President William Taft of the United States was moved to say that "the Emperor of Russia has passed workers' legislation which was nearer to perfection than that of any democratic country." The people of all races in the Russian Empire had an equality of status and opportunity, which was unparalleled in the modern world. His Imperial Majesty Tsar Nicholas II (1894-1917) and his state bank had created a worker's paradise that was unrivaled in the history of mankind. (Goodson, 87-89).

There is no mystery here. The equally autocratic German emperor passed similar legislation a bit later. In both cases, economic growth in both agriculture and industry averaged 15% yearly. Population growth boomed, and, in the Russian case, peasants were given free land and tools in lush, southern Siberia (not the frozen north) for the sake of colonizing this vast empty space about twice the size of the US. By 1905, 90% of Russian arable land was in the hands of peasants. No other industrialised society could match this. Peasants were buying noble land in massive quantities as Russia, at the same time, was completely self-sufficient. Her domestic market accounted for almost 99% of her production, and she needed nothing from abroad. All she got from the West was revolution.

Moving southward, Georgia requested Russian protection as a shield against her Islamic neighbors. The XIII Dalai Lama of Tibet, Thoubten Gyamtso, requested Tsar Nicholas II to take his country under Russian protection to protect this Buddhist monarchy from drowning in British opium. Several Russians served as tutors to Tibetan nobles and the Dalai Lama himself. Russia was seen as the Savior of all who fought British and Chinese imperialism.

Tsar Nicholas II was tempted to make war on Manchu China, since China held the western Buddhist populations and the Tibetans in thrall. Several million Muslims also were held under Chinese Manchu rule. Russia was called the "White Savior" long prophesied by Chinese sages. Making matters worse for the British, oil was discovered in Baku, today's Azerbaijan, then part of the Russian empire. The Rothschild dynasty declared war on Russia, financed Russian revolutionaries and importantly, created an anti-Russian alliance.

The Rothschild alliance, for their part, was created in retaliation for Russian success. It was based on financing Turkey, the Turkish tribes of the Russian south, Persia, and, most ominous of all, Japan. Turkish occupation of the Balkans was given the Rothschild's seal of approval since, without Turkey, pro-Russian states like Serbia and Bulgaria would fill the vacuum. The British press praised the Turks as liberators from "Orthodox superstition" and held the Russians to be "Mongols" whose "fangs" must be kept out of the Balkans.

Russia helped finance Bulgaria and Serbia, and sought to unify China once the Manchu state fell. With an indirect protectorate over Tibet and the addition of the literate and urbanized Georgian state, an unstable balance of power between the banker's paradise and the worker's paradise was reached. Unfortunately, Japan was a much better bet than China. Russia supported Afghanistan against England in the Anglo-Afghan war of 1879-1880, but this was not as significant as the recreation of Japan under the aegis of the Royal Navy.

Had Russia not been a party to World War I, what might the world look like as a result? A realistic scenario could look like this: The exploding Russian population would have populated all Siberia and parts of Central Asia. She would have taken the Balkans and Constantinople, quite possibly with Germany's blessing. This would have permitted Russia's taking of most of the Middle East, or at least acting as the chief protector of the Orthodox Greeks and Arabs. Germany would see the rationality in an alliance with Russia over Vienna. Russian and German interests, ideology and political systems were quite similar. The Russian alliance with her old enemy England made little political sense for Russia, but controlling German expansion was London's priority by 1910-1913. Germany realized that her alliance with Austria-Hungary would force Germany into any conflict Vienna might back itself into. This would not be in Germany's interest. Austria's poor military performance in the war, as well as her unstable economy, is what forced Germany to divide its military forces between two fronts.

Russia's new and growing oil wealth, her immense natural resources, internal market and industrial capital would have financed a protectorate over all China and quite possibly southeast Asia. Much of Central Asia, under Chinese control, would have also come under Russian protection, if not occupation. Compared to English colonialism, Russian expansion was never exploitative, but defensive.

This market, economic growth and continued population explosion would have drawn the remaining powers of the world to Russia. She would be seen as, militarily speaking, unassailable. Moving east instead of west, she would be no threat to the European balance of power. Any alliance with Germany would seal the nature of Europe as a strong traditionalist, royalist and Christian land power. Vienna would be worse than helpless, and might begin to unravel as the Germans of the empire sought union with Germany and the Slavic population looked to Russia. An angry and expansionist Hungary would be also helpless, constantly at war with her equally angry minorities.

The Orthodox church would find a willing ally in (royalist) German Lutheranism and the growing Old Catholic movement. Had Russia and Greece joined with this schism from the Roman church, as originally planned, the Old Catholic Church would have grown substantially. There was already quite an interest among conservative Anglicans and some Lutherans in the Orthodox tradition.

Much of western Canada would have come under Russian control from the population of Alaska, whose positive interaction with the native Aleutians made Russia a welcome presence, rather than an imperial one. Russian firms were already in Hawaii, and would have protected the monarchy there. The US financed the Hawaiian royal house's overthrow. Given Russia's welcome in much of Asia, there is no reason to believe the Hawaiian royal house (and other Pacific states) would not also see the benefit in a powerful, yet distant, protector.

Russian imperialism was not profit seeking as the British empire was. It was defensive. Native populations were normally treated well, and, as in the case of the Armenians and Muslims of Asia, never were forced to convert to Orthodoxy or speak Russian. They took their oath to the Tsar on the Koran. Poland was granted one of the most liberal constitutions in the world, and Finland, another colony of Russia, was totally independent in every respect except foreign policy. Hence, there is no reason to hold that Russian imperial rule would have been resented, or even have been considered "rule" in the normal sense.

Today, this seems like a fantasy barely conceivable. But for a time, prior to the mass slaughter of World War I, this was considered a viable reality in St. Petersburg and London. Goodson gives a glimpse as to why this might have been:

In 1860 The State Bank of the Russian Empire was founded with the aim of boosting trade turnovers and the strengthening of the monetary system. Up to 1894 it was an auxiliary institution under the direct control of the Ministry of Finance. In that year it was transformed into being the banker of the bankers and operated as an instrument of government's policy. It minted and printed the nation's coins and notes, regulated the money supply and through commercial banks provided industry and commerce with low interest rate loans (Goodson, on Alexander II, 83-84).

The opponents of the Pax Russica were not idle. St. Petersburg, for all its problems, was one nut the banking regime could not crack. If Russia continued its massive development, population growth and industrialisation, usury would be destroyed. The Russian state, more so than private capital, planned and directed investment with local funds. The French were the only substantial foreign presence in Russian industrialism. If this was to be replaced with Russo-German joint projects, usury would be under severe attack. Something had to be done. To give the reader a hint what this was, Goodson quotes Congressman LT McFadden's speech to the House of Representatives in 1932:

They [western banks] financed Trotsky's mass meetings of discontent and rebellion in New York. They paid Trotsky's passage from New York to Russia so that he might assist in the destruction of the Russian Empire. They fomented and instigated the Russian revolution and they placed a large fund of American dollars at Trotsky's disposal in one of their branch banks in Sweden so that through him Russian homes might be thoroughly broken up and Russian children flung far and wide from their natural protectors. They have since begun the breaking up of American homes and the dispersal of American children. (Goodson, 116-117).

McFadden was silenced. Mr. Goodson likewise. Your author lost an academic post for it. There is no issue like usury, and no power that can conceivably match that of compound interest. The left is the product of the banks, and much of the neocon "right" is as well. Monarchy was overthrown in its interest and replaced with a global oligarchy controlling, depending on the source, upwards of 80% of global GDP. All of this exists, of course, in the name of freedom, progress and democracy.

We began this lengthy essay with the concept of usury and western banking being quite comfortable with radical left statism. We have come full circle, explaining how and why this demonic alliance has come to pass. It remains with us today, and the opposition to it remains anemic. Yet, it is not as if there is no reaction, however vague, to the continued monopolization of wealth and labour.

Goodson does not end on a negative note. North Dakota is how Goodson ends his work. As if the reader needs more proof of the destructive tendencies of usury and fractional reserve finance. North Dakota established a state owned bank in which the revenues of the state are deposited. It provides low interest loans to farmers and small businesses. All profits revert to the state. Without the normal practices of compound interest charged against the citizen, North Dakota has not been affected by the real estate debacle of 2007. State GDP has grown by almost 100% since 1997, while personal income per capita has grown by about 140% in that same time frame.

While the media has been quick to argue that North Dakota's success is exclusively due to its small petroleum industry, this kind of development has certainly not occurred in Alaska, which has far more oil than North Dakota. Nigeria is drowning in oil, and yet, she remains poor. Somalia and Chad, too, have rivers of oil, as do Indonesia and Burma, but all of these states also remain poor. Apparently, oil only benefits North Dakota and the Beverly Hillbillies.

Indeed, the central strength of Goodson's book is its consistency. It has one thesis: wherever state banks rule the financial universe of an economy, that economy does very well. His analysis of 1930s Germany, Italy and early 20th century Japan all feature state controlled banks, low interest loans, state directed investment and a general loathing of libertarian free markets. They also feature triple digit growth rates, zero unemployment and low inflation. In our own day, China, Taiwan and Belarus all are in the same boat.

Belarus, as Ukraine and Russia floundered once the IMF and Harvard University helped the Mafia rig privatization deals, saw its President, Alexander Lukashenko, halt privatization, centralize power, and nationalize finance. While Ukraine today has lost 70% of its industry and sees 80% of its well educated population below the poverty line, Belorussian unemployment is 1% and her industry has grown by an average of 10% yearly since 2000. The two Chinas likewise: when George Soros engineered the Asian currency meltdown of 1997, the only two economies unaffected were the two that had state-controlled banks, Taiwan and China. Former powerhouses like South Korea and Japan, as well as Thailand, became official wards of the IMF. Their lifetime employment was abolished, and living standards have fallen.

Prior to the wars that ravaged both states, Libya and Syria were also registering double digit yearly growth, popular presidents and both countries were closing in on first world status. Both countries had state controlled banks and state-directed investment. The state was a partner in investment, not the result of it. Saddam Hussein's Iraq was doing the same until the US engineered the war with Iraq.

The Burmese state bank is under the control of the Ministry of Finance, headed by Major-General Hla Tun with a western education in finance. His deputy is Colonel Hle Swe. Clearly, the Burmese are taking no chances with foreign manipulation of their currency. Burma's oil, rich soil, minerals, close ties with China, and its educated population are increasingly making it a target for western speculation, as well as political attacks. Given that country's civil war, western sanctions and separatist movements, she still has managed to build 10 universities, several dozen dams, increased literacy to 80% and ensured that peasants own their own land since 1999. If the reader has detected a pattern, then he is correct.

Goodson's work, of course, is not flawless. It's errors, however, are minor. He holds that Gavrilo Princip was Jewish, and that his assassination of the Archduke Ferdinand started World War I. Princip was not allegedly Jewish, especially since he came from the backwater of western Bosnia, in the poor peasant village of Obljaj, which is totally rural and inaccessible. He was the child of poor peasants of Bosnian Serb stock. His mother's maiden name was the very Orthodox Misic. Neither his father nor mother have Jewish names, and his father's lowly job in the postal service does not scream "banking elitist." Princip was part of the "Young Bosnia" group, loosely connected to the military society "The Black Hand," also known as "Unification or Death." This was a nationalist organisation of military men that had no connection with the few Jews living in Serbia at the time. His extended family is Jovicevic, from Montenegro, where nary a Jew has ever tread.

The assassination of Ferdinand did not start World War I. Serbia acceded to the demands of Vienna after the assassination, and Germany too, was impressed of the Serbian desire for peace. Serbia was completely exhausted from the Balkan Wars and could not fight yet again. Furthermore, the choice of target makes little sense: Ferdinand was more or less popular among the southern Slavs, as he was seen as the most pro-Serb of the royal family.

Austria, on the other hand, was itching for a *casus belli* ever since the local rebellion against her occupation of Bosnia and artificial creation of the "state of Albania," which served to cut Serbia off from the sea and separate Montenegro from Serbia proper.

The circumstances of the Grand Duke's visit were odd. Ferdinand was visiting Serbia and Bosnia on the Serbian national day, *Vidovdan*, when nationalist tempers were high. This was also the beginning of highly inflammatory military manoeuvres in Bosnia. Ferdinand lacked the normal security detail for royals visiting hostile territory. Ferdinand's motorcade was inexplicably rerouted by his own Austrian people, where Princip and some others were waiting. Yet, much to Germany's chagrin, even before the Serbian answer to the Austrian ultimatum was received, Vienna had declared war.

These two errors are really of no significance, but they are common and understandable errors that needed to be addressed. These in no way detract from the immense accessibility and utility of this book, which deserves wide dissemination. For what it's worth, I endorse the work of Mr. Goodson whole-heartedly.

Matthew Johnson PhD
Fayetteville
Pennsylvania

Review by Tom Sunic

In the European popular consciousness money has traditionally been associated with something dirty, something criminal, something unworthy of European man, something taught to be savored and excelled at only by secretive foreigners and distant aliens. From Antiquity to Post-modernity tons of books have been written on the subject of cursed money and wretched gold. One needs to recall the scenes from the ancient Greek King Croesus, or the wretched Midas gold, or think about the mass slaughter in the medieval Niebelungen saga whose story revolves around hidden gold in the Rhine River and the suffering caused by that gold.

Well, as Stephen Goodson reminds us in his book, neither have the obsession with abstract money, nor the practice of usury, and the role of gold, lost much of their deadly flavor today. In fact many modern business transactions and many global financial malpractices, spurred by the greed for gold, have become even deadlier, threatening this time around not just the survival of Western civilisation but the whole of mankind.

First off one must make it clear that Goodson is not an adept of conspiracy theories, nor is he a Jew-baiting scribe whose prose often inflicts more harm than good to a reader wishing to enlighten himself on the subject of fictitious money and its not so fictitious creators. For that matter Goodson can sport his top notch references regarding the subject matter which he analyses in his book; he was a Board member of the SARB (South African Reserve Bank) with long experience in banking business, or to put it less prudishly, he was a first-hand observer of insider trading business. How is it possible that in our so-called best of all the democratic world, a world which boasts transparency and a free judiciary, most citizens haven't got the slightest clue as to who are the shareholders of major central banks, such as the Federal Reserve Bank in the USA and many other banks world-wide? Goodson demonstrates how in fact the famed American Federal Reserve has nothing to do with state property or the meaning of democracy in the USA, but serves instead as an anonymous corporation, as a crime syndicate of powerful financial movers and shakers. It is certainly no accident that ever since the explosion of the so-called housing bubble in the USA in 2008, not a single major banker, be it from Goldman Sachs, be it from J.P. Morgan, has been called to account for printing false money or handing out surreal loans. One hand washes the other—one might say.

From Goodson's book transpires a remarkable knowledge of social and political circumstances of ancient Rome, or for that matter Cromwell's England, or Weimar Germany. Therefore, his book cannot be dismissed as just another boring piece in the mosaic of silly anti-Semitic and conspiratorial literature which one often encounters among many right-wingers. It is precisely Goodson's dispassionate narrative, well embedded in the framework of different historical periods which makes his book not just an informative and scholarly literature, but also a refreshing read for a novice wishing to find out more about the mystique of money.

Usury seems to have been for ages at the heart of social upheavals and wars. The ancient Romans experienced its blows many times, which ultimately lead to Rome's demise. Goodson portrays the Roman statesman Caesar's social and economic reforms, his introduction of the first welfare system, the remission of rents for many destitute Roman citizens, and finally Caesar's interdiction of charging interest on the already existing credit interest. The Roman Empire briefly flourished. Many aristocrats, however, could not tolerate Caesar's magnanimity towards the poor and decided to kill him. Usurers, of whom many were foreigners of Jewish origin, alongside their fawning Gentile lackeys, seem to have been the major transmission belt in the growth of corruption and decline of Western civilization.

Similar patterns of economic growth and decline could be observed during the drafting and adoption of the famed Magna Carta in medieval England whose prime goal was to cancel the bonds of the earlier Jewish moneylenders and to abolish usury. Indeed, several decades later, in 1290, the implementation of Magna Carta was followed by the expulsion of the Jews from England. A cautious reader may justifiably ask the question as to why so many classical authors, let alone illiterate European commoners, have throughout the ages blamed the Jews for all social and economic ills and why have Jews been so often victims of savage persecutions? Far from engaging in hate speech or vilifying the Jews the author correctly documents the inordinate percentage of Jews in the moneylending business, a detail which has historically contributed to their own tragic fate.

Neither does the author circumvent the power of new political and theological ideas, notably the rise of early Calvinism and the birth of the new mindset among the 16th and 17th century European and American politicians and opinion makers. Calvin's teachings about predestination and the important social role model he had assigned to the merchant had a huge impact on political life in Europe and in the newly discovered America. The merchant and the usurer, became, so to speak, the new role models in high politics and finances, somebody worthy of emulation, somebody to be used as a superego by Gentiles. This Gentile mimicry of Jews, via early Calvinism and Puritanism, spread rapidly, first in early capitalist America and later, particularly after the Second World War, in continental Europe. Goodson notes how the 16th century English revolutionary and Calvinist fanatic, Oliver Cromwell, thought of himself as a "chosen one", and not just as an ordinary Shabbat goy. Soon after the beheading of King Charles I, Cromwell reopened the gates of England for the warm welcome of the Jews.

The author also throws an interesting light on the quality of life of commoners in late medieval England, a country in which in many aspects the quality of life was superior to the quality of life in our modern societies. In the 14th and 15th century, English commoners worked less than 14 weeks per year. If we were to judge happiness and the quality of life only by the number of electrical appliances and our bank accounts, we'll never be able to understand the real meaning of happiness. In many instances, however, the so-called dark ages in England and continental Europe looked much brighter than our own dark age. Much of the church architecture of that time was the direct expression of popular joy, where the quest for spiritual transcendence was far more in demand than the fleeting bliss of the modern system in which money hoarding has become a new secular religion.

And then came the bad news. In 1694, the Bank of England was created, the model on which all central banks in Europe and later in the USA was replicated. Soon thereafter started, what modern academics call, "modernity", which in reality meant reducing people to servitude. English big time financiers did not like the fact that early US colonies had issued their own money and showed hostility to the Bank of England. The attempt of England at abolishing US currency was also the prime cause of the American Revolution. To a large extent 19th century America prospered precisely because of the absence of a central bank. One must not forget, as the author states, that Andrew Jackson's presidential campaign was carried out under the banner "VOTE ANDREW JACKSON, NO BANK!" The ominous year for the USA, as well as for the entire world was the creation of the Federal Reserve Bank in 1913, which indirectly precipitated the Western world into two world wars and hundreds of local wars all over the world.

Nor was the situation rosy for American citizens. Although becoming much envied citizens of a global superpower, since 1919 until 2014, the US national debt has skyrocketed from US$2.6 billion to US$17.5 trillion. Nobody wants to publicly state it, but most American and Western citizens live not a life on credit, but rather thrive and vegetate with their death on the instalment plan. The time of the mega crash and the end of the white race may be just around the corner.

The author describes similar fiat money and different forms of banking, wheeling and dealing in other parts of Europe, as well as the rise of Bolshevik Russia, largely financed by the Jewish New York bankers. The merit of his book is that he does not look at the banking environment in a black and white fashion but always searches for some shading in between. It is commendable that Goodson also mentions the German economist Gottfried Feder, who was himself one of the most outspoken critics of usury and compound interest in Weimar Germany. The problem though with the name "Feder" is that this renowned economist was also for some time affiliated with National Socialism, which may unquestionably raise some eyebrows and red flags even among the most dispassionate readers of Goodson's book. How can one today, in our politically correct and self-censored academic environment, extract from some early national socialist scholar something positive? National Socialism, being today officially depicted as the symbol of absolute evil must never contain something that might be accepted as relatively good—even in apolitical fields such as sport, ecology, let alone economics. Feder, based on his study of heavy reparation monies Weimar Germany had to pay to the victorious side after WWI, had come to the conclusion that paying compound interest would impoverish citizens and result in mass unemployment. Feder's teaching could be applied today, especially if one considers possible remedies in tackling the huge sovereign debt of all Western countries combined.

In a somewhat less pessimistic note the author mentions the amazing success of the US state of North Dakota, whose bank has enabled North Dakota to become the most dynamic state with the lowest unemployment rate in the USA. How North Dakota will weather the storm in years to come remains to be seen. As long as main stream academics and the media hesitate to tackle the root causes of the incoming financial chaos, the USA, along with its Western satellites, will likely be heading from one disaster to another.

Dr. Tomislav Sunic
Zagreb
Croatia

Bibliography

D.J. Amos, *The Story of the Commonwealth Bank*, Veritas Publishing Company Pty Ltd, Bullsbrook, Western Australia, 1986.

A.N. Andreadēs, *History of the Bank of England*, P.S. King & Son Ltd, London, 1935.

D. Astle, *The Babylonian Woe*, Private Edition, Toronto, 1975.

D. Astle, *The Tallies, A Tangled Tale and The Beginning and the Ending*, Private Edition, Toronto, 1997.

P.T. Bauer, *Equality, and the Third World, and Economic Delusion*, Harvard University Press, Cambridge, Massachusetts, 1981.

I. Benson, *The Zionist Factor*, The Noontide Press, Costa Mesa, California, 1992.

K. Bolton, *Stalin, The Enduring Legacy*, Black House Publishing Ltd, London, 2012.

K. Bolton, *The Banking Swindle - Money Creation and the State*, Black House Publishing Ltd, London, 2013.

W.D. Bowman, *The Story of the Bank of England*, Herbert Jenkins Ltd, London, 1937.

E. H. Brown, *Web of Debt, The Shocking Truth About Our Money System and How We Can Break Free*, Third Millenium Press, Baton Rouge, Louisiana, 2008.

G. Buchanan, *My Mission to Russia and other Diplomatic Memories*, Cassell and Company Limited, London, 1923.

H.S. Chamberlain, *The Foundations of the Nineteenth Century*, The Bodley Head, London 1912, Vol. II.

K. Chazan *The Jews of Medieval Western Christendom 1000-1500*, Cambridge University, New York, 2008.

A. Cherep-Spiridovich, *The Secret World Government or "The Hidden Hand"*, The Anti-Bolshevist Publishing Association, New York, 1926.

O.P. Chitwood, *John Tyler Champion of the Old South*, Russell & Russell, 1964.

F. Chuev and A. Reis, *Molotov Remembers*, Chicago, 1993.

J.H. Clapham, *The Bank of England: A History 1694-1914*, Cambridge: The University Press, 1914.

G.M. Coogan, *Money Creators, Who Creates Money? Who Should Create It?*, Omni Publications, Hawthorne, California, 1963.

I.M. Cumpston, *Lord Bruce of Melbourne*, Longman Cheshire, Melbourne, 1989.

W. Cunningham, *The Growth of English Industry and Commerce during the Early and Middle Ages*, Cambridge University Press, 3rd edition, 1896.

L. Degrelle, *Hitler Born At Versailles*, Vol. I of the Hitler Century, Institute for Historical Review, Costa Mesa, California, 1998.

A.J de Grund, *Fascist Italy and Nazi Germany: The 'Fascist Style of Rule'*, Routledge, London, 2004.

A. Del Mar, *The History of Money in America From the Earliest Times to the Establishment of the Constitution*, Omni Publications, Hawthorne, California, 1936.

A. Del Mar, *Money and Civilization: Or a History of the Monetary Laws and Systems of Various States Since the Dark Ages and Their Influence upon Civilization*, Omni Publications, Hawthorne, California, 1975.

E. de Maré, *A Matter of Life or Debt*, Humane World Community, Inc., Onalaska, Washington, 1991.

R.E. Elletson, *Monetary Parapometrics: A Case Study of the Third Reich*, Christian International Publications, Wilson, Wyoming, 1982.

S. Fay, *Portrait of an Old Lady*, Penguin, London, 1987.

G. Feder, *The Program of the NSDAP, The National Socialist German Workers' Party and its General Conceptions*, translated by E.T.S. Dugdale, Fritz Eher Verlag, Munich, 1932.

N. Ferguson, *The House of Rothschild, Money's Prophets 1798-1848*, Vol. 1 and Vol. 2, Penguin Books, London, 1999.

G. Ferrero, *Greatness and Decline of the Roman Empire*, Vol. VI, William Heinemann Ltd, London, 1908.

A.N. Field, *The Truth About The Slump – What The News Never Tells*, Privately published, Nelson, New Zealand, 1935.

A.N. Field, *All These Things*, Omni Publications, Hawthorne, California, 1936.

I.N. Fisher, *Stamp Scrip*, Adelphi Publishers, New York, 1933.

J.K. Galbraith, *The Age of Uncertainty*, Houghton Mifflin, Boston, 1977.

T.H. Goddard, *History of Banking Institutions of Europe and the United States*, H.C. Sleight, New York, 1831.

R. Gollam, *The Commonwealth Bank of Australia: Origins and Early History*, Australian National University Press, Canberra, 1968.

O. and J. Grubiak, *The Guernsey Experiment*, Distributionist Books, London, 1992.

A. Hitler, *Mein Kampf*, Hurst and Blackett, London, 1939.

Hitler's Table Talk, compiled by M. Bormann, Ostera Publications, 2012.

J.A. Hobson, *The War in South Africa, Its Causes and Effects*, James Nisbet & Co., Limited, London, 1900.

D.L. Hoggan, *The Forced War: When Peaceful Revision Failed*, Institute for Historical Review, Costa Mesa, California, 1989.

E. Holloway, *How Guernsey Beat The Bankers*, Economic Reform Club & Institute, London, 1958.

R.K. Hoskins, *War Cycles – Peace Cycles*, The Virginian Publishing Company, Lynchburg, Virginia, 1985.

F.J. Irsigler, *On The Seventh Day They Created Inflation*, Wynberg, Cape, South Africa, 1980.

D. Irving, *The War Path: Hitler's Germany 1933-1939*, Macmillan, London, 1978.

Money and Banking in Japan, the Bank of Japan Economic Research Department, translated by S. Nishimura, edited by L.S. Presnell, Macmillan, London, 1973.

E.M. Josephson, *The "Federal" Reserve Conspiracy & Rockefellers*, Chedney Press, New York, 1968.

H.S. Kenan, *The Federal Reserve Bank*, The Noontide Press, Los Angeles, 1968.

A. Kitson, *A Fraudulent Standard*, Omni Publications, Hawthorne, California, 1972.

G. Knupffer, *The Struggle for World Power, Revolution and Counter-Revolution*, The Plain-Speaker Publishing Company, London, 1971.

Bibliography

R. Kraus, *Old Master Thereof, Jan Christian Smuts*, E.P. Dutton & Co. Inc., New York, 1944.

J.M. Landowsky, *Red Symphony*, translated by G. Knupffer, www. archive.org/details/RedSymphony

The Letters of T.E. Lawrence edited by D. Garnett, Jonathan Cape, London, 1938.

C.A. Lindbergh, *The Economic Pinch (Lindbergh on the Federal Reserve)*, The Noontide Press, Costa Mesa, California, 1989.

D. Marsh, *The Bundesbank: The Bank That Rules Europe*, William Heinemann Ltd, London, 1992.

E.S. Mason and R.E. Asher, *The World Since Bretton Woods: The Origins Policies, Operations and Impact of the International Bank for Reconstruction*, Brookings Institution,Washington D.C., 1973.

'*Collective Speeches of Congressman Louis T. McFadden*', Omni Publications, Hawthorne, California, 1970.

S. McIntyre, *A Concise History of Australia*, Cambridge University Press, Melbourne, 2009.

S.S. Montefiore, *Stalin: The Court of the Red Tsar,* Weidenfeld & Nicolson, London, 2005.

N. Mühlen, *Hitler's Magician: Schacht The Life and Loans of Dr Hjalmar Schacht*, trans., E.W. Dicks, George Routledge & Sons Ltd, London, 1938.

E. Mullins, *The Secrets of the Federal Reserve*, Bankers Research Institute, Staunton, Virginia, 1993.

C.S. & R.L. Norburn, *A New Monetary System Mankind's Greatest Step*, Omni Publications, Hawthorne, California, 1972.

T. Pakenham, *The Boer*, Jonathan Ball Publishers, London, 1979.

J. Perkins, *Confessions of an Economic Hitman*, Plume, New York, 2005.

E.N. Peterson, *Hjalmar Schacht: for and against Hitler: A political economic study of Germany, 1923-1945*, The Christopher Publishing House, Boston, 1954.

"Ezra Pound Speaking" Radio Speeches of World War II, Edited by L.W. Doob, Greenwood Press, Westport, Connecticut, 1978.

P.J. Pretorius, *Volksverraad, Die Geskiedenis agter die Geskiedenis*, Libanon-Uitgewers, Mosselbaai, Western Cape, South Africa, 1996.

The Protocols of the Meetings of the Learned Elders of Zion, translated from the Russian text by Victor E. Marsden, former Russian correspondent of "The Morning Post", London, 1934.

Muammar Al Qathafi, *The Green Book*, Public Establishment for Publishing, Advertising and Distribution, Tripoli, Libya.

C. Quigley, *Tragedy and Hope A History of the World in Our Time*, The Macmillan Company, New York, 1966.

A.H.M. Ramsay, *The Nameless War,* Britons Publishing Co., London, 1952.

R.V. Remini, *Andrew Jackson*, Twyne Publishers Inc., New York, 1966.

J. Robison, *Proofs of a Conspiracy against all the Religions and Governments of Europe, carried on in the Secret Meetings of Free Masons, Illuminati, and Reading Societies, collected from Good Authorities*, Western Islands, Belmont, Massachusetts, 1967.

J.E.T. Rogers, *The First Nine Years of the Bank of England*, Clarendon Press, Oxford, 1887.

A. Rosenberg, *The Myth of the Twentieth Century*, The Noontide Press, Torrance, California, 1982.

R. Rudman, *England Under The Heel Of The Jew,* https://www.scribd.com/document/73734255/England-under-the-heel-of-the-Jew

J. Ryan-Collins, T. Greenham, R. Werner, A. Jackson, *Where Does Money Come From, A Guide to the UK Monetary and Banking System*, New Foundation, London, 2012.

R.S. Sayers, *The Bank of England 1891-1944*, Cambridge University Press, 1976.

W. Scott, *The Life of Napoleon Bonaparte* Volume II, University Press of the Pacific, Stockton, California, 2003.

R.E. Search, *Lincoln Money Martyred*, Omni Publications, Palmdale, California, 1989.

W.G. Simpson, *Which Way Western Man?*, Yeoman Press, Cooperstown, New York, 1978.

F. Soddy, *Wealth, Virtual Wealth and Debt*, G. Allen & Unwin, London, 1933.

O. Spengler, *The Decline of the West*, The Modern Library, Random House, New York, 1932.

N. Starikov, *Rouble Nationalization The Way to Russia's Freedom*, St Petersburg, Piter, 2013.

Bibliography

T.L. Stoddard, *Into The Darkness: An Uncensored Report From Inside The Third Reich At War*, Ostara Publications, Burlington Indiana, 1940.

J.G. Stuart, *The Money Bomb*, William Maclellan (Embryo) Limited, Glasgow, 1984.

A.C. Sutton, *Wall Street and the Bolshevik Revolution*, Arlington House Publishers, New Rochelle, New York, 1981.

V. Suvorov, *The Chief Culprit Stalin's Grand Design to Start World War II*, Naval Institute Press, Annapolis, Maryland, 2008.

I.Tarbell, *A Short Life of Napoleon*, S. S. McClure Limited, New York, 1895.

A.J.P. Taylor, *The Origins of the Second World War*, Hamish Hamilton, London, 1961.

H.A. Thomas, *Stored Labor: A New Theory of Money*, 1991.

G.M. Trevelyan, *English Social History, A Survey of Six Centuries Chaucer to Queen Victoria*, Longmans Green and Co., London, 1948.

Verheimlichte Dokumente – Was den Deutschen verschwiegen wird, Fz-Verlag, Munich, 1993.

L. Villari, *Italian Foreign Policy under Mussolini*, Holborn Publishing Ltd, London, 1959.

T.E. Watson, *Sketches from Roman History*, The Barnes Review, Washington, DC, 2011.

N.H. Webster, *The French Revolution*, The Noontide Press, Costa Mesa, California, 1982.

J. Weitz, *Hitler's Banker Hjalmar Horace Greely Schacht*, Little, Brown and Company, London, 1999.

R.G. Werner, *Princes of the Yen*, M.E. Sharpe, New York, 2003.

R. McNair Wilson, *Monarchy or Power*, Eyre & Spottiswoode, London, 1934.

F.P. Yockey, *Imperium*, The Noontide Press, Torrance, California, 1983.

Index

Continental Blockade 60
Continental dollar 67
Crime of 1873 77
Cromwell, Oliver 35-38
Cunningham, Dr. William 26
Currency Bill 66

D
Dark Ages 22, 175
De Medina, Solomon 40, 46
Deutsche Arbeiterpartei 134
Deutsche Bundesbank 147-148
Deutsche Mark 147
Deutschnationale Volkspartei 137
Deutsche Reichsbank 140, 147
D'Israeli, Israel 25, 34
Dodge, Joseph 155
Dorislaus, Isaac 37
Douglas, Clifford Hugh 122-125, 150, 178
Dreikaiserbund 93

E
Earl of Anglesey 38
East India Company 166
Eckstein, Hermann 97
European Central Bank (ECB) 148
Edict of Milan 21
Edward I 27-28
Edward VI 32
Edward the Confessor 25
Elizabeth I 33, 160
Elleston, Roger 139
Etruscans 11, 13

F
Feder, Dr. Gottfried 131-134
Federal Reserve Act 117-118, 120
Ferdinand, Archduke Franz 101
Ferdinand II of Aragon 33
Field, A.N. 40, 108, 114-115
First Bank of the United States 46, 70, 166
First Name Club 81
First National Bank of New York 81

Strong, Benjamin 110
Sulla, Lucius Cornelius 20
Sutton, Prof. Antony 90
Swiss Federal Council 109
Sword Blade Bank 165

T
Tally sticks 29-30
Tarquin the Proud 11
Taylor, A. J. P. 147
Taylor, Colonel Dick 76, 179
Tecumseh, Chief 70
Temple of Juno Moneta 14
The Chicago Plan Revisited 127
Theodosius, Emperor 21
Tiberius, Emperor 16
Titus Tatius 11
Tojo, Prime Minister General Hideki 154
Treaty of Commerce of 1911 153
Treaty of Tilsit 58, 60
Treaty of Utrecht 53
Treaty of Versailles 106, 141, 147
Trevelyan, George Macauley 31
Tripartite Pact 154
Trotsky, L. 101, 116
Troubled Asset Relief Program (TARP) 168-169
Tyler, President John 75

U
United States Federal Reserve Act 117-118, 120
United States Federal Reserve Bank 74, 115-116, 119
United States Federal Reserve Bank of New York 108
United States Federal Reserve Board 111, 116, 119-120

W
Wall Street Plan 79
Wall Street Reform and Consumer Protection Act 169
Warburg Bank 82
Warburg, Paul Moritz 79, 81
War of the Spanish Succession 53
War Hawks 72
Wernher, Beit & Rothschild 97
William III 40

Lightning Source UK Ltd.
Milton Keynes UK
UKHW02n2324270418
321788UK00009B/45/P

9 781910 881637